The Reinvention of Marketing

Deborah Malone

Volume 2014, Number 1

the internationalist PRESS

The Internationalist Marketing Series is supported by The Internationalist and the ANA

THE INTERATIONALIST PRESS
New York • London

ISBN 978-1-942324-00-3

This book is dedicated to a marketing industry in transition —one that is dramatically evolving to become a more thought-provoking, critically-important, and meaningful business discipline. It also honors the men and women who are assuring that it stays true to its purpose and affects positive change for both business and consumers alike.

Table of Contents

RETHINKING Accepted Notions of Branding Building

TRANSFORMATION as an Essential Way Forward

CHALLENGING the Status Quo to Create New Frameworks

PURPOSE: Instilling Purpose through New Actions

LEADERSHIP: New Views of Marketing Leadership

Foreword

Today's marketing ecosystem has one never-ending constant. And that constant is "evolution." We are in an environment where change happens dail—fueled largely by the "technology revolution" of real time marketing, mobile, social, programmatic buying and so much more.

This revolution is so, so important to the marketing community. It has given us the opportunity to reframe our relationships with consumers and customers—forging dialogue and exchanges that provide abundant enlightenment about each other. By knowing what's on each other's minds, we can create marketing strategies that leverage core insights to fuse longer lasting bonds and generate brand value based on loyalty and friendship.

The Reinvention of Marketing 2014 is a transformative compilation of brand and business insights from around the world. These insights capture the evolution brand by brand—and company by company. It is a fresh look at how these marketing enterprises cope with evolution. It demonstrates how they pivot to leverage new found consumer understanding while applying new tools and metrics to better measure the outcomes of their efforts.

This wonderful compilation chronicles the various, diverse journeys of brand marketers—from purposeful branding to new approaches to measure ROI. It is reflective of why these superb authors and brand

champions are recognized in the prestigious **INTERNA-TIONALIST 1000.** This global group is identified with broad scale success in their efforts to establish long term growth and demonstrable business results. The Reinvention of Marketing 2014 celebrates their success and provides insight and instruction for all—as we navigate our pathways to similar championship.

At the ANA, we look to reference points that benchmark our respective journeys and provide milestones for how well we are succeeding. It is fundamentally clear that the *Reinvention of Marketing 2014* is one of those pivotal collections that give us the refreshing clarity we all need and desire. I trust you will find some golden nugget that will enlighten you as it has enlightened me.

Bob Liodice
President & CEO
Association of National Advertisers—ANA

Acknowledgments

Yes, it does take a village to write a book about *The Reinvention of Marketing*, and many acknowledgments are in order.

First, I must sincerely thank all of the chapter collaborators—those marketing leaders with non-stop schedules who have contributed their time and brain power simply with the good intentions of moving an industry forward through their shared experiences. My conversations with Morten Albæk, Dana Anderson, Barbara Basney, Pete Blackshaw, Zita Cassizzi, Fernando Chacon, Jesper Colding, Carmen d'Ascendis, Jason Hill, Amy Lou, Nadine Karp McHugh, Lee Nadler, Clayton Ruebensaal, Simon Sproule and Joe Tripodi have helped me better understand the industry's direction and its key touchstones. They have all significantly influenced my own thoughts about marketing's very vibrant future.

I am grateful to the ANA/Association of National Advertisers and its dynamic President & CEO Bob Liodice for believing in **THE INTERNA-TIONALIST 1000** initiative—*1000 Marketers Around the World Reinventing Marketing* and for being such a strong champion for the collaboration between **The Internationalist** and his exceptional marketing organization. Bob, along with ANA folks like Duke Fanelli, Bill Duggan, Kathleen Hunter, Lan Phan and Barry Garbarino (now at Collective), have all helped to shepherd so many of our joint programs for marketers. *The Reinvention of Marketing* would not be possible without the support of those partners initially responsible for insuring that **THE INTERNA-TIONALIST 1000** project got off the ground. They include: John Williams and Carolyn Gibson of the BBC; Charlie Whittingham of BrightRoll; Daniel Rothman of the *Financial Times*; Perry Kamel of Elateral; Stephanie Fierman of MediaCom, Shane Cunningham, John Toth and Emily Dalamangas of Reuters; and Sebastian Jespersen of digital agency Vertic, Inc.

Last, but certainly not least, I must thank my stalwart Internationalist supporters—Brendan Banahan and Peggy Bloomer—for coping with late nights, early mornings, missed meals and little vacation. Finally, a shout-out (*Woof! Woof!*) to the Vizsla duo, Rosie and Annie, for insisting that I go for walks, and not sit in front of side-by-side computers for hours on end.

The Reinvention of Marketing

To say that marketing has changed is an understatement. In the 20+ years that I've been involved with this business, I've seen marketing evolve—dramatically. Yet, the acceleration of the last several years can aptly be defined as "reinvention." Those working to harness this change should be proud of the renewed industry they are creating.

Not only is marketing more critical now to every organization, but it can literally do good, transform brand and consumer relationships through honesty and passion, and even change the world. (Heady stuff, but you'll find some amazing ideas in the following chapters of how marketing can actually make a world of difference.)

There's no question that today's always-on, accountable, social media environment has radically shifted the rules of "doing good business." Responsibility and transparency are now central to how any brand or business plays its proper role in society.

More companies are embracing big, sustainable ideas that demonstrate true marketing innovation in an effort to deeply connect with customers' passions and values. These ideals are simply CENTRAL to new marketing principles. When done right, business growth is often a result, and this new way of working truly represents a global revolution in marketing intentions and possibilities.

Marketing's transformation, of course, is also a result of technology, globalization, and shifting economics. Considerations about "the reinvention of marketing" are essential navigational guides as the industry looks to deliver purpose and meaning to brand values in a business world increasingly defined by social media, mobility, analytics, "big data," return on investment, new leadership standards, and the need for global growth.

Fifteen individuals, who have spent the majority of their adult lives in marketing, have shared the realities and visions of their efforts in this business. Given the rich diversity of brands represented, it is also remarkable to see an alignment of immediate objectives and future directions. No one was tasked with a specific subject to consider; all simply shared their perspectives, and each vignette emerged. Interestingly, at this moment in time, their thoughts resonated with five key contemporary issues:

- RETHINKING Accepted Notions of Branding Building
- TRANSFORMATION as an Essential Way Forward
- CHALLENGING the Status Quo to Create New Frameworks
- PURPOSE: Instilling Purpose through New Actions
- LEADERSHIP: New Views of Marketing Leadership

There are others like them and more who have been inspired by Morten Albæk of Vestas Wind Systems, Dana Anderson of Mondelēz International, Barbara Basney of Xerox, Pete Blackshaw of Nestlé, Zita Cassizzi of TOMS, Fernando Chacon of Itaú Unibanco, Jesper Colding of Mengnui, Carmen d'Ascendis of Brown-Forman, Jason Hill of GE, Amy Lou of

Hauwei, Nadine Karp McHugh of Colgate-Palmolive (and soon L'Oreal USA), Lee Nadler of MINI, Clayton Ruebensaal of Ritz-Carlton, Simon Sproule of Tesla and Joe Tripodi of Coca-Cola. And in future annual editions of The Reinvention of Marketing, we'll do our best to find them and share their ideas with the world.

RETHINKING
Accepted Notions of
Branding Building

Lee Nadler

Shares How Passion Is at the Heart of MINI's Powerful Image

Lee Nadler

Marketing Communications Manager

MINI USA (division BMW)

Woodcliff Lake, New Jersey USA

FAST FACTS
Where were you born?
New Rochelle, New York

Was there a lesson you learned in an early first job that still applies now?
My first job was as an account person at a WPP-owned promotions agency. I worked hard and after two years was put in charge of an assignment that was seen as small to most people. Given that it was the first initiative which I "owned", I was excited and I made it important by finding opportunities that others ignored. I developed an idea, sold it into the client and it became a showcase piece of business for the agency. The lesson is that when people feel empowered and a sense of ownership for initiatives they work on, sometimes they can do amazing things.

What is the best advice you were ever given?
When things don't go well, it's not failure. It is often part of the process and can lead to a different, perhaps better path.

Are you willing to admit your biggest career mistake? (Or at least the one you learned the most from!)
In 1995 I decided to quit my job at agency Kirshenbaum & Bond to work for a non-profit group, The Shoah Foundation. I was inspired by the mission and involvement of Steven Spielberg. My role was to develop a major project for them in six months. Only after I had accepted the job and quit my current job, did we work through the plan together. The directors, who two weeks earlier hired me by saying "let's do it," were suddenly scared that the project would overwhelm them and killed the project. Now they said, "Can you get your other job back?" The mistake was that I should have outlined all of the key requirements and assumptions that would need to be met to make the project successful, before taking on the role.

Where do you turn for inspiration?

I have learned a lot from the Sherpa community, while trekking in the Himalayas. The Sherpa spirit and determination often inspire me, which I write about on my blog, www.TheSherpaPath.com.

What's your favorite city for business travel?
Tokyo

What's your favorite place in the world?
NYC

LEE NADLER HAS BUILT A SUCCESSFUL CAREER BY RECOGNIZING WHAT makes a brand special. At MINI—without question a very special brand—he performs his role best by tapping in to the passion of MINI owners, many of whom call themselves "MINI-acs," and by inviting other young-at-heart individualists to become part of the MINI community. A car with an immediately-recognizable personality that is clever, fun and cheeky, MINI's remarkable DNA translates to an oversized and enormously powerful brand asset.

Interestingly, MINI achieves its magnetism without a level of marketing expenditure normally associated with dynamic, strong-selling auto brands. MINI consistently punches above its weight in a myriad of ways.

Lee Nadler's role as MINI's Marketing Communications Manager has taught him a few unexpected lessons. One includes managing the tricky balance between upholding the brand's core values while embracing owners' needs for personalization. (MINI enthusiasts have a deep emotional connection with the car; roughly half admit to naming their vehicle.) Lee calls this a "willingness to take 'hands off the wheel' and let a customer have a say, and then do something." MINI has gone so far as to create a model that's designed by owners.

Another marketing lesson is understanding the MINI Mindset. Lee refrains from describing MINI owners by specific demographics, but instead recognizes a psychographic profile comprised of people who are adventurous, individualistic, open-minded, creative, tech-savvy, and young at heart. And this Mindset is consistent throughout the world.

So what's MINI's secret? And how does Lee channel this remarkable brand enthusiasm to keep all communications and activations fresh, current and MINI-like?

Lee jokes that MINI is the only car that comes standard with friends. And MINI repeatedly proves how its devotees see fellow owners as "extended family," a feat few brands accomplish. Central to the MINI ethos is a strong emphasis on engagement with owners and on its motoring community. In fact, just this summer, the entire MINI USA executive team, most with their families, along with legions of passionate owners, embarked on an amazing motoring adventure called MINI TAKES THE STATES, a biennial event that the company has run since 2006. For two weeks (July 26-August 9), MINI owners from around the world participate in a truly epic transcontinental road rally from San Francisco to Boston with stops in 18 cities over the course of 15 days.

The origins of the rally began when several dozen MINI owners decided to drive coast-to-coast in an informal convoy. This year's MINI TAKES THE STATES included over one thousand enthusiasts in a single segment. MINI motorists have the option to join the cavalcade for a portion of the trip like Albuquerque to Lubbock, Dallas to Memphis, Chicago to Cleveland, Bethlehem to Boston, or they can partake in the entire cross-country journey, as did Lee and 350 new friends.

MINI owners and rally participants are passionate—to the point, for example, that they've convinced their entire running club to buy the cars. Some are in owner clubs, like the MINIskirts, with chapters around the world and a devotion to raising money for various causes. This year's MINI marathon also included over 100 pets on the journey. In fact, Banfield Pet Hospital was a MINI TAKES THE STATES partner— connecting drivers with their locations throughout the tour, and confirming their mission is to enrich the family-pet relationship. Plus, MINI USA named Best Friends Animal Society® as the charitable partner for the 2014 rally.

MINI TAKES THE STATES also has a significant number of sponsors and partners from InterContinental Hotels Group, Liberty Mutual, Sirius to candy-maker Peeps from Bethlehem Pennsylvania, who created a Peeps MINI for the stop in their hometown. Lee and the Peeps team first met at the 2013 ANA Masters of Marketing conference and subsequently put the partnership together.

MINI owner and actor Tony Hawk, considered to be one of the most successful and influential pioneers of modern vertical skateboarding, kicked off the 2014 MINI TAKES THE STATES tour by jumping his board over MINIS as they started on the journey. (Hawk, incidentally, is now 46 years old—the same age as the average MINI owner in the US... although demographics aren't the critical factor in MINI's marketing.)

Lee Nadler also understands that driving, or motoring in the MINI lexicon, is an individualistic experience. (Despite the fun of road trips, only one driver at a time can experience the thrill of driving a MINI.) Yet, the brand has created a community built on something individualistic. This key insight extends to MINI's marketing principles, particularly in regard to sponsorships. Instead of sponsoring team sports, the brand embraces activities that are individualistic-- yet where a fun and energetic community and culture have been built. You'll find MINI carving mountain roads and slopes at the Burton Mountain Festival and US

Open Snowboarding Championships or as the presenting sponsor of the Channel Islands (CI) Demo Tour, which invites the surfing community to join an event at their local beach and try out the latest CI surfboards and gear. The company created a MINI Boat to open the Head Of The Charles Regatta®, the world's largest two-day rowing event in Cambridge, Massachusetts, which soon turned spectators' surprises into smiles.

MINI's Olympics sponsorship at the London Games included remote-control quarter-scale electric "mini- MINIs" on the playing field of the stadium to transport and return javelins, shots and discuses to competing athletes. MINI seamlessly became part of the fun and the action—not in an interruptive way, but as an "invited guest." Lee recognizes, "There was a time when sponsorship meant that you could pay your way into the party. But will that insure that people will share and engage with your brand?"

MINI has certainly created a brand ethos that's fun, original and clever. When headlines and conversation about the approaching date of the predicted Mayan apocalypse became prevalent, MINI ran a witty ad entitled, "Well, So Much For The 2014 Models." It stated: "So, if the world ends today in accordance with Mayan prophecy, you pay nothing. Ever." The following day, another ad appeared: "We're Still Here." And added: "But in light of the world not ending, you will have to make the payments."

Of course, MINI also represents how an extraordinary brand can be reintroduced with a new relevance and freshness that creates a movement. And BMW has been very good about understanding what MINI initially symbolized when introduced in 1959 in the UK and how that spirit is alive today.

The original MINI came of age during a time of creative revolution and self-expression. It became a symbol for an independent spirit, while integrating the fun and practicality of a small car. Interestingly, by experimenting with technology to turn the engine on its side, MINI became a revolutionary small car that was big inside—big enough for a family. And a wider wheel base enabled superior handling making it fun to drive. Its design created a lot of fans. When people saw it on the road, it was surprising, but immediately friendly and inviting. It was a product to which people were drawn.

John Cooper then tinkered with MINI to make it a performance racing car. It also became the little car that could. Even while winning, it had an underdog spirit that rallied people.

Many of these core values from the early days continue to exist. The car still puts a smile on your face. It has the underdog spirit, the British cheekiness, and it's playful, fun. The MINI brand continues to be the MINI brand. When BMW reintroduced the car a dozen years ago, it evolved better performance, but kept the DNA.

Everything at MINI begins with investing in the relationship with its owners and recognizing that people who own a MINI have a true personal connection with their car and the brand. Lee often asks when speaking at marketing conferences, "How many of your customers would have the kind of relationship with your product or service where they would actually name it or invite it into their life in some special way?" He adds, "We don't take it for granted. Such loyalty is among our greatest brand values."

As a result, MINI invites people to share their voice and their stories. Concurrently, the company strives to listen, learn and communicate with a brand voice that is distinctly MINI. Nadler admits, "Being connected to our owners keeps us on our toes."

One example of listening and leveraging its customer enthusiasm resulted in the 2014 Cooper Hardtop. Lee tells the story of a competition that asked MINI owners to not only customize the Cooper Hardtop design online, but also recommend ways the car could be tested prior to its launch. In other words, before MINI would officially introduce the car—and before dealers get to drive it—they would ask owners to test it. "This strategy," he said, "represents a huge departure. Traditionally, a new car is brought to the dealers. It's brought to the auto shows. There's a press event. Dealers have a party to invite current owners and new prospects. But MINI has brand love, and we put owners first."

MINI's marketing is continually seeking the best way to engage with owners and adopting the tools they are using. There is a constant, real time relationship between the brand and its customers. Many MINI owners are engaged through social channels, as well as through clubs and rallies. MINI seeks to include the brand in relevant conversation by looking at what's happening in the world, what's happening at MINI, and then assessing what's germane to its core attributes—all in an effort to better connect with owners and relate to new customers. They evaluate not only what messages are "liked," but are commented on and shared as it is a better indication of how well they're connecting with owners, followers and fans.

When Lee Nadler considers what changed most in marketing, he's quick to point out: "The walls have broken down—the connection from consumer to brand and brand to consumer is now direct. This has a multiplier effect on messages as they now have a wider range than ever before. Technology allows us to share and connect. It also allows consumers to play with content, and ultimately allows people to see what they want. It levels the playing field."

He adds, "Many talk about 'real time' marketing, and there are interesting ways to keep your finger on the pulse now. However, is it possible for companies and agencies to create communications in ways that are speedy enough to go through the process of necessary approvals—and within a certain level of acceptable production standards? Or do you give consumers a voice and allow products to be essentially used in ways you don't control? It's hard for companies to get their head around this. The good ones shine. A brand can stimulate the conversation or sit passively on the sideline. We choose to stimulate."

Over a 20+ year career, Lee Nadler has lead marketing for several successful companies and initiatives, including: DoubleClick which he joined in 1996 as its' first head of marketing and then establishing DoubleClick Japan and Australia; launching new products and partnerships for BMW; creating unique promotions for Snapple; penetrating new markets for Yahoo!; shaping the presentation for NYC to host the Super Bowl; and recently expanding the brand platform for Gilt Groupe.

Lee has also built and led two marketing agencies/firms. He was CEO of Digital Pulp until late 2001, one the leading digital marketing agencies in the US at the time. Sherpa Marketing was formed in 2002 to collaborate closely with great companies and inspiring individuals to reach their Summit of Success.

In May 2012, Lee joined the BMW Group as Marketing Communications Manager for MINI. He is responsible for managing unique, multichannel, MINIcentric marketing programs in US. He oversees MINI's three agencies and has overall responsibility for: online and offline advertising creative & media; MINIUSA.com on all platforms, digital/video marketing, social channels, multicultural marketing and research. He lives in NYC with his wife and daughter and currently Motors in a tricked out 2014 MINI Countryman Cooper S nick-named "Bluepee Oreo."

Beyond his functional expertise, Lee has gained a unique perspective by learning from Sherpas, on two trips to the Himalayas, including a month long trek to Mt. Everest in 2012.

It started in 1998 when he was invited on an Expedition with other marketers who provided pro-bono advertising to the non-profit Outward Bound. They trekked through the Annapurna foothills of Nepal with Sherpa guides. That experience opened Lee to the unique Sherpa culture and spirit. And it provided a fresh perspective that he incorporated into his life and business.

Among those Sherpa principles are: Leading with quiet confidence. Commitment to team. Sense of purpose. Positive energy. Calm during tense situations. Acceptance of mistakes. Perseverance. Selflessness. Compassion. Trustworthiness. And laser-like focus on achieving a goal. The principles have become Lee Nadler's guideposts. He maintains a blog at www.TheSherpaPath. com.

Carmen d'Ascendis

Explains How to Keep an International Brand Relevant…
When Relevance Is Increasingly a Moving Target

Carmen d'Ascendis

*Managing Director for Finlandia
Vodka and Chambord Liquor*
Brown-Forman
Amsterdam, The Netherlands

FAST FACTS
Where were you born?
I was born and raised in New Jersey

*Was there a lesson you learned in an
early first job that still applies now?*
It's better to be generally correct and
on time than perfect and late

*What is the best advice you were ever
given?*
Have a point of view. Luck is for the ill
prepared.

What was your big career break?
Probably my first international assignment

*With an intriguing long-term career with Brown-Forman, what advice do you have
for other marketers in terms of staying engaged within an organization?*
Patience with a willingness to relocate.

*As a truly global marketer and internationalist who has lived in many countries,
what are some the most significant brand lessons you've learned from around the
world?*
People are more alike than different; yet we spend more time debating
the differences.

What's your favorite city for business travel?
Anywhere I can walk for hours and enjoy the culture, architecture and cuisine.

What's your favorite place in the world?
The dinner table with my wife and children.

CARMEN D'ASCENDIS BELIEVES THAT THE CHIEF TASK OF A MARKETER "is to make brands relevant and imbue them with meaning." He explains, "When someone places a bottle of Finlandia Vodka on a table or when someone calls the brand by name in a bar, it says something about that person. It says that he is a person who follows his own path, preferring to have a life less ordinary."

He admits that this marketing undertaking isn't easy. "Relevance is a moving target. What is relevant to a 25 year-old today is different from what was relevant to a 25 year-old five years ago. Too often we hold on to messages and programs for too long. This is borne from fear; fear that we will alienate our core consumer, and fear that if we change, we will mess up something."

Carmen d'Ascendis' deep thinking about contemporary marketing issues and keen instincts about successful global branding combine with a life-long passion for the business. With more than 22 years in a diversity of roles at Brown-Forman, one of the top 10 global spirits companies, he is a marketing leader who brings wisdom and experience to the profession.

He understands that relevance, perhaps the most critical component of brand affinity, only takes on more significance in an always-on and constantly-shared social media world. For d'Ascendis, the role of a good marketer is to simultaneously provide ways to be relevant to tomorrow's consumers while keeping today's enthusiasts devoted to the brand. This can mean targeting Millennials without isolating other generational groups. Although he says a constantly-evolving, "cool" brand rarely loses its devoted fans.

He adds, "Contrary to popular belief, millennial customers embrace brands and brand messages. The abundant use of brand hash-tags on Instagram is just one sign of the consumer's efforts to associate themselves with a brand's meaning. Our challenge is to give our brands meaning before the consumers do."

Carmen d'Ascendis believes, "The most gifted brand builders are also great storytellers. Telling the brand's story provides context and meaning, which is something consumers seek. Storytelling is more than a marketing luxury; it is good for the bottom line. Successful storytelling separates brands from commodities; it supports premium pricing and helps brands endure."

Storytelling at its best is also rich, complex and multidimensional. "What draws someone in to a brand is not what keeps them there." He differentiates "gateway values" that initially attract people to a brand from core "retention values" that build loyalty. "And you need both messages in the environment to keep consumers interested." As brand fans learn more and go beyond superficial reactions, they discover new layers that help them grow closer to the brand.

"Building relationships with consumers is like building relationships with friends," he says. "The more you get to know someone, the closer to them you grow. For brand builders, storytelling is the best way to do this. But a simple, one-way monologue is not enough in the Age of Social; we need to show how our story relates to the consumer and close the gap on why they should care."

In fact, Carmen d'Ascendis believes that the constantly changing nature of our Digital Age has only served to reinforce his conviction that "as marketers, we are storytellers first and foremost."

So how do these issues of relevance work on a complex global level with varying brand positions by country and differing levels of local marketing expertise? As a global marketing leader, Carmen d'Ascendis' role requires him to connect the dots of disparate data points in culture and draw conclusions on how this information will impact his business in the future, while country marketers are charged with developing programs that drive profitable growth in the near-term. By working together along this marketing continuum we are able to build strong brands.

Nonetheless, when considering how he determines the success of marketing efforts to drive sales, Carmen is characteristically eloquent: "I like to think I am using art in the service of commerce." He adds, "Relevance cannot be measured solely by the number widgets sold. And traditional continuous tracking studies, with metrics like 'for people like me,' are blunt instruments that lack meaning. A successful campaign makes a brand part of the conversation. So in addition to units sold, I look at equity scores, memes spawned, and spoofs inspired."

Although his role may be to establish consistent global brand assets, Carmen d'Ascendis is realistic when recognizing local nuance. "Of course there is flexibility by country," he says. "After all we need to be relevant."

He admits, "We worked very hard, alongside our creative partners, Wieden + Kennedy, to develop the Finlandia Vodka and Chambord Liqueur creative strategies and core creative ideas. These positions were only established after various rounds of research to understand the why's, how's and where's of the brand and its consumers, and completed prior to developing any creative work.

We also conduct research after the work is completed, or on air, with a vision to evolving the creative. Local flexibility comes in the articulation of the strategy. Symbols of luxury, or premium, or less ordinary, vary by region. If we want our message to be understood, we must on occasion alter the symbols we employee."

Prior to Finlandia and Chambord, Carmen d'Ascendis was the Director of Marketing for Jack Daniel's, a 146-year old brand with a strong

American heritage that found it had resonance in over 150 countries. He saw the core values of the brand as rich and multi-layered enough to be strongly relevant outside of the US. He says, "There were so many things I was able to draw on— craftsmanship, small-town values, entrepreneurship and the self-made man, and rock and roll rebellion. The challenge was matching the options with consumer motivation, something that varied by region and over time. I remained surprised and have the deepest respect for the passion of the brand loyalists – the tattoos, the self-governing community in social media, and the depths of their thirst for brand knowledge."

Without question, global brand success takes both experience and vision—strongpoints for d'Ascendis. He says simply: "While the 'expression' or relevant messaging changes, the 'DNA' of the brand doesn't. Evolving the messaging to be relevant with the tenor of the times is essential."

When talking to his teams around the world, he often discusses relevance in terms of the James Bond franchise of the last 50 years. "The franchise is strongest now even though there have been six different men who have portrayed Bond. Those six characters match the tenor of their time; the flawed hero of SkyFall would not have worked in the fantastically, futurist time of Moonraker. Each character adapted, while keeping true to the essence of Bond."

He adds: "What's relevant is always evolving. Don't protect a brand from evolution. It's a mindset change from defense to offence."

Another key global issue for d'Ascendis is reconciling the two most frequent comments he hears around the world: "share best practice" and "my market is different." He is convinced that "Finding the sweet spot between these two opposing thoughts helps us keep our brands relevant regardless of geography." His work to resolve this issue has led him to the belief that "adopting good practice" is the more appropriate and the more difficult task. He says, "Sharing best practice is easy; it's just bragging about the work you do. Whereas adopting good practice requires us to recognize similarities between markets and spot the program element that will work in our market."

He recognizes that the programs and activities a market develops are done so to address a particular set of circumstances. "It is unlikely that this same set of circumstances exists in another market. So taking a 'best practice' from one market and parachuting it into a second market is unlikely to deliver the same result. We need to find the best pieces of the program that will have resonance in our market."

The phrase, "best practice" suggests it's the only way of doing something, and if it's the best, evolution is not required. "When referring to these activities as examples of good practice," he explains, "we open possibilities and allow our teams to draw inspiration from their colleagues." And Carmen d'Ascendis is not interested in simply sharing such ideas, but tasking his people to actually adopt them. That brings freshness, relevance... and results.

He knows first-hand how a team of ambitious marketers around the world feeds this process of adoption and evolution. "A powerful tool in evolving the message and keeping the brand relevant is recognizing that some local marketers will be more experimental or adventuresome than others." His challenge is to encourage those who are less daring to adopt these "outside" ideas.

"I would certainly characterize 'innovation' as a requirement for success. I'm not speaking of product innovation but innovation in communications."

Without doubt, Carmen d'Ascendis believes this is a very exciting time to be in marketing. He is even enthusiastic about the fragmentation

of the media landscape, which he views as the most significant difference he's seen in marketing during his 20+ year career. "Today we have
the ability to fragment our communications. In fact, we can fragment our
message to build a deeper brand experience. We can use each medium
for what it's best suited; film and TV to build emotion, followed by more
rational information as we get closer to the point of purchase. We can
leverage the strength of each medium to do its job now and target more
deeply by better understanding individual messaging."

He admits, "Probably my biggest mistake as a marketer was failing
to recognize earlier the combined power of social media and hashtags.
Together they transform WOM (word-of-mouth) into C-to-C (consum-
er-to-consumer) marketing. I initially saw social media as a nice way to
tell brand stories. I thought it was a sideline to more elaborate produc-
tions-- often operating in isolation and meandering without purpose.
To me, Hashtags were an afterthought, slapped on at the end. Today
social and hashtags are a vital part of our digital strategy, working in
tandem with our dot.com. Social gives us the opportunity to introduc-
tion ourselves and invite people in for a closer look. It also facilitates
an exchange between us and our fans-- making them part of a larger
community. Hashtags are the shareable nuggets that help people join
the conversation on a global stage."

There's no question that Carmen d'Ascendis cares deeply and
thoughtfully about his craft. So where does he turn for inspiration? He
says, "I am an external thinker. I also like to walk so I find inspiration
at the nexus of these two things. I look forward to and occasionally
plan trips to places like New York, London and Tokyo so my marketing
director and I can walk for hours and talk about what we see and what
we are doing."

Carmen d'Ascendis has lived in eight cities on four continents while working in 50 countries on behalf of Brown-Forman. Today, he's based in the company's European headquarters in Amsterdam as the Managing Director of Finland Vodka and Chambord Liquor, a role he took on in spring 2014.

In fact, his extraordinary career with Brown-Forman started 22 years ago when he entered the business as a merchandising representative. Forget statistics that measure the tenure of chief marketing officers in intervals of months, Carmen underscores how curiosity, creativity, adaptability lead to success with longevity.

His roles and geographies demonstrate a process of brand experience and thought leadership that few achieve. Carmen's own roots in are in the US, not in Lynchburg, Tennessee—the famous home of Jack Daniels, but in the East Coast state of New Jersey. However, he is unquestionably a true citizen of the world.

His international Brown-Forman career began in the late '90s in London as Area Manager of Duty-Free for Europe and Scandinavia. He then relocated to Germany to take on his first country-specific Marketing Manager role. That soon led to a new assignment and a new continent when he became Regional Director of Australia and New Zealand. His next transfer took him to Japan as the country's Commercial Director where he delivered the two best financial years in that market's history. While based in Tokyo, Carmen took on the additional role of Brand Director for Jack Daniel's Asia Pacific and uncovered consumer insights that led to the redevelopment of Jack Daniel's Single Barrel as the new "face" of the JD trademark.

He then returned to the US—to the company's Louisville, Kentucky headquarters-- to use his international experience as Global Brand Director of the Jack Daniel's Ready-to-Drink business around the world. He worked closely with country teams in markets as varied as Mexico, Japan and Germany to develop market-specific offerings.

His role prior to the recent move to Amsterdam was Director of Global Marketing for Jack Daniel's. This included the highly successful launch of the Jack Daniel's Tennessee Honey line extension, the "Barrel Tree" campaign that brings family and friends together, a new responsive-designed web site that adapts to any device from smartphone to tablet to computer, and a doubling of the brand's volume growth rate. Carmen was named an **Internationalist of the Year** in 2012 for these efforts.

Jason Hill

Shares How GE Has Moved from Advertiser to Publisher of Content on a Global Stage

Jason Hill
Director of Global Media Strategy
GE
New York, New York USA

FAST FACTS
Where were you born?
Highland Park, IL – the North Shore
suburbs of Chicago

*Was there a lesson you learned in an
early first job that still applies now?*
A mentor at my first agency job
(Saatchi & Saatchi) encouraged me
to approach every task, even paper
clipping a presentation for the client, as an opportunity to do something quickly and
thoroughly, proving value to others. It was a good reminder that you don't get bigger
responsibilities until you've mastered the smaller ones.

What is the best advice you were ever given?
"Only you are responsible for your career"

What was your big career break?
Joining the new business team at Saatchi 18 months into my advertising career. It
was a huge boost, giving me exposure to management and a role in the most scruti-
nized projects at the agency—both good motivations to work hard.

What's your favorite city for business travel?
Hong Kong. The ability to order lunch via free airport train WiFi to the office while
en route from another on-time Cathay flight makes it hard to beat for ease and
convenience!'

What's your favorite place in the world?
As much as I love to travel, always great to be home in NYC

GE OFTEN REFERS TO ITSELF as the "world's oldest start-up" given its continual application of innovative thinking and technology to solving contemporary challenges. Jason Hill, GE's Director of Global Media Strategy, has been applying similar thinking in his approach to the company's growth markets around the world, and has not only discovered a number of eye-opening lessons about what it takes to be global today, but is also at the forefront of exploring how brands and content navigate in today's fast-changing world.

In fact, Jason has recently returned from spending 6 months in Asia, based in Hong Kong, so he could "get under the hood" to better understand the marketing and media landscape there first hand. The Asia Pacific region is of increasing importance to GE, while its digital media ecosystem is quite different from that of the United States and much of Western Europe.

GE, of course, is one of the world's best-known brands and highly-regarded companies with businesses that span the fields of energy, health and home, transportation and finance. With a footprint in over 100 countries, GE's marketing underscores its global leadership role—whether through green technology (ecomagination), healthcare (healthymagination), or "Brilliant Machines" with an emphasis on advanced manufacturing, Big Data, and the industrial internet.

Jason's work is focused on developing a global media program with an emphasis on those international markets with the greatest growth potential for GE. Fifteen key countries and sub-regions across six continents are considered top growth markets; they vary tremendously by culture and media trends, and include Australia, Brazil, Canada, China,

Germany, India, Indonesia, Malaysia, Myanmar, Turkey, Saudi Arabia, Sub-Saharan Africa, UAE, and Vietnam.

Despite the diversity of these nations and geographies, GE's marketing message strikes a chord throughout the world by focusing on big, human stories about technology and innovation that are broad enough to include conversations about jet engines or CT scanners. Jason calls this focus on innovation "a north star" which helps to shape global media programs-- both at scale and with flexibility to key markets.

His goal is not only to drive brand familiarity and commercial activity through GE's advertising and communications, but it is to lead program development with agency partners, media owners, content publishers, and platforms. GE has been aggressive about experimenting with evolving forms of content development, storytelling, and new media. For example, they were the first brand on Vine, the short-form video-sharing service, and their #6SecondScience continues to be retweeted and reposted. They have also been early adopters of other social properties, so Jason continually seeks out areas of innovation in paid, shared, and earned media for the company's brand content, content creation, and integrated programs with top global media companies.

He says, "We have a mandate to develop marketing initiatives that are as innovative as the products coming out of our global R&D centers. So we experiment; we take risks; we want to look at channels that make sense to our audiences to craft strategic and breakthrough ways to use those channels."

The "Look Ahead" program is one example of effective and engaging content that demonstrates how one of marketing's biggest brands has turned its advertising model upside-down to provide thought leadership to the difficult-to-engage business leader community around the world by providing a GE perspective on a myriad of issues from energy to healthcare.

"Look Ahead" is a first-of-its-kind partnership with The Economist Group to produce a daily article, video, slideshow or infographic, and seed it in franchise positions around economist.com. It's a view of technology and innovation through the lens of GE, but is rarely about the company as GE's goal is to provide valuable content, not repurposed press releases.

"In terms of the role of content, one thing our reputation research tells us—and we do a lot of it—is that the more people know GE, the more they like GE. So our content strategy is about uncovering and telling great stories about innovation, technology, big data, developing healthcare, and so on. We want our customers, our shareholders, our employees to know what GE thinks about the world and content-led programs are a way to do it."

In fact, when Jason discusses the *reinvention of marketing*, he underscores how our digital media world has enabled all messages to become global, while, simultaneously, all things global must now become digital. "This is the biggest change for brands and how they go to market." He adds, "As digital media and social networks have grown up, they have fostered globalization, a democratization of content, and a greater sense of connectivity across markets than we've seen before." He believes that this has transformed client, agency and media relationships forever. "The old partner characterizations are all disintermediated. Traditional boundary lines have become completely porous."

He adds "As a marketer, we now have to be content creator, platform and distributor. For example, the exchanges from GE Garages- an initiative to reinvigorate interest in invention, innovation and manufacturing that enables participants to work with technical experts and partners in a "fab lab"—are now housed in GE Reports, the company's daily online magazine, and distributed through the GE social channels."

Jason believes that many marketing organizations assume that having "global" brands simply means sales and distribution of their products in other countries with a TV commercial translated into another language. "While this definition has become more sophisticated, many marketers have yet to evolve their thinking. Brands must commit to global; they must think and act in borderless ways—from their strategic insights, to their creative campaigns, to how they plan and buy media. At GE, we began investing in our global brand one country at a time in conjunction with our sponsorship of the Olympics. The positive response from local market customers and employees was instantaneous, and we quickly ramped up our efforts in key markets around the world. We've learned a lot along the way, and we're only just beginning."

Jason offers the following as advice, or what he prefers to call "thought-starters," to consider when building a global brand:

DNA is universal

Define a direction for your brand that crosses company borders and comes from the core of who you are. If your business strategy is sound, there will be remarkable consistency in how stakeholders view their relationship to the brand across cultures. Nowhere is this better expressed than among employees.

Boots on the ground

When it comes to developing messages and making them relevant to local audiences, a global brand team can't live in a hometown bubble. Frameworks and structures help, but local market nuances must guide the approach. And nuances don't come through over the phone—you have to get out and see it for yourself.

In country for country or go home

Your brand can only be as local as your business. If you don't have localized production, manufacturing, employment, there's no point in trying to tell a local story. Credibility is paramount. And it's not just for marketing. Revenue opportunities go to the companies who have committed major sunk costs. We like to say that it's not about what GE means to the market but what the market means to GE.

State of the union

In developing markets, business strategy and growth areas are increasingly shaped by government priorities. Understanding national objectives, getting close to government, and shaping brand communications to match is crucial. Your closest partner for understanding the market may be your government relations team.

Paid meets earned—one team with shared objectives

Global audiences, especially business decision makers, have already filtered the content they want to consume. When it comes to news and information, brands aren't going to curate it for them, but are better placed to integrate, convene, and shape the conversation in real time—acting like a publisher. Tap into the entourage effect and pair with media brands who share a common DNA. This means marketing and PR must be connected at the hip.

Redefine the creative process

Acting like a publisher applies to creative development and production, too. Global brands need to take a nimble, always-on approach to gathering and distributing content. We suspect the agency model looks more like a news organization with a few bureaus than a map with hundreds of dots, like those we put up in pitch meetings ten years ago.

Innovate, incubate, scale

These are the three steps we follow, particularly when it comes to our media partnerships and content activities. The social web means campaigns are no longer discrete or walled-off, and content must be made to ricochet, not just for added eyeballs, but because global brands need to tell a globally consistent story. Another lesson: don't just innovate and incubate at home, wherever that may be. Our best pilots have been in non-U.S. markets where the tollgates are more frequent and more unfamiliar. We have had more success with scale when we pilot in a challenging place.

"All of these points," he says, "have implications for team structure, agency relationships, and talent. Indeed, balancing a desire for scale and the necessity of nuance is a challenge, but one well worth under-taking, and one that will become ever more central to advertising in the latter half of this decade."

Although Jason has shared this advice with Wharton's 2020—Future of Advertising program, he has additional lessons from his recent six months in Asia, particularly in terms of consolidating creative efforts to be more consistent and efficient. He admits that he now looks to Asia for the next wave of media innovation, rather than thinking he could export his current ideas of innovation to Asia. For example, when he consid-ers China, he now recognizes the rate at which people are consuming content, how their preferred platforms are local to China, and what the country's scale and engagement online can mean for GE programs.

Without question, GE rallies around moments of science and tech-nology; in fact, the company cares about "owning moments"—from the relevant to the micro-relevant. In doing so, they have expanded their definition of content and reoriented their focus to emphasize what's most relevant to their customers. Not only have they proven that b-to-b is far from boring, but they show how it can also be personal—even if it's about big technology, solving big problems, and dreaming big. GE's latest "Childlike Imagination" project operates at the nexus of storytelling and dreaming big, while demonstrating how GE scientists are taking childlike imagination and making it fantastically real—all through the eyes of little girl whose Mom works at GE.

Jason Hill recognizes that great content, combined with the right time and place, then amplified through conversation, should speak louder than any "ordinary" media program. However, it requires working with both speed and courage—particularly when a company like GE is always in motion, which means the brand in always in motion. However, change is increasingly part of any brand ethos, just as marketing is a multifaceted function. Or as Jason so aptly summarizes, "Invention and innovation are at the heart of GE and its 130 year history. It also has to be central to our marketing."

Jason Hill joined GE in June 2011 as the Director of International Advertising & Content. In 2012, he was simultaneously named an **Internationalist of the Year** *by* **The Internationalist** *and received an* **ANA Rising Marketing Star Award** *through nominations by senior executives who consider these individuals as role models for the industry's workforce. .In February 2014, his role expanded to Head of Global Media Strategy.*

He began his career on the agency side of the business. Jason had two roles at Bartle Bogle Hegarty New York while it was named Agency of the Year three times consecutively by the 4As—one was the Director of Business Development, and the other was Account Director and Founding Member of ZAG Brand Invention, a new BBH business unit aimed at creating brands from scratch and partnering with investors and manufacturers to take them to market.

His first agency role was at Saatchi & Saatchi in both Business Development and Account Management.

Jason holds a B.A. in Political Science from Northwestern University and an MBA from Yale. He is a frequent speaker at industry conferences including

ANA Content Marketing Conference, Advertising Week New York, Festival of Media Asia, and Monetizing Media London. He has contributed thinking to the Wharton Future of Advertising Program and Columbia Business School's Global Communications Forum.

TRANSFORMATION
as an
Essential Way Forward

Pete Blackshaw

Outlines Nestlé's Digital Transformation to Build Brands and Delight Consumers

Pete Blackshaw

*Global Head of Digital Marketing &
Social Media*
Nestlé S.A.
Vevey Switzerland

FAST FACTS
Where were you born?
Detroit Michigan

*Was there a lesson you learned in an
early first job that still applies now?*
Marketing only matters if you close the
sale.

What is the best advice you were ever given?
Go to business school. Ironically, this advice came from my former boss and mentor,
Art Torres, then a California State Senator. He knew my "marketing skills" as his
press secretary and legislative aide had potential well beyond politics. I will always
be grateful.

What was your big career break?
Getting a summer internship at P&G. This put me on an irreversible marketing path.
The second was re-entering the corporate world with Nestlé a few years ago. Abso-
lutely fascinating global experience.

*Are you willing to admit your biggest career mistake? (Or at least the one you
learned the most from!)*
In 2000, I raised $31 million to start an early version of TripAdvisor or Yelp.com, but the
model ended up pivoting to a different business model. While I'm proud of the eventual
outcome – we ultimately were acquired by Nielsen – I regret not being able to make
the original model work. I probably would have done a few things differently.

What's your favorite city for business travel?
I absolutely love my trips to Milan. Only three hours by train from our global headquarters in Switzerland. When in US, you can't beat San Francisco or New York.

What's your favorite place in the world?
I have a deep emotional connection to my home town of Pasadena, California. My
roots are everywhere in that city, and every trip is special.

IN HIS ROLE AS NESTLÉ'S GLOBAL HEAD OF DIGITAL MARKETING & SOCIAL MEDIA, Pete Blackshaw is helping to lead change within the world's largest food company, and in doing so, is also reshaping contemporary attitudes toward marketing's power and value. Throughout his career, Pete has served as a marketer, an entrepreneur, a digital guru, an author, a data analyst, and a community service leader. Much of his success is tied to how he often manages to effortlessly juggle these roles simultaneously, while taking their best attributes to form an enduring vision. Although these varied disciplines may initially appear to be unrelated, all underscore his relentless drive to use the tools of the Internet to empower individuals and change the status quo.

His role as tireless champion of today's digital world is now benefiting Nestlé, the world's largest food company, as it embraces transformation to become a leader in leveraging digital and social media to build brands and delight consumers. Pete's arrival in Vevey roughly 3 years ago corresponded with Nestlé's goal to become the #1 fast-moving consumer goods player in leveraging digital to more effectively build brands that deeply connect with consumers.

Not only is this ambition a top priority, but Nestlé recognizes just how much is at stake. Worldwide, the company sells approximately 1.2 billion products every day, and an increasing percent of this volume is tied to digital links. Every day, the company produces over 1,500 pieces of original content across its 850 Facebook pages. And now, 200,000+ Nestlé employees are part of a collaborative internal social media network.

Pete notes that Nestlé understands how digital is as much an operating principle, as it is a communications channel. This is significant. He emphasizes that digital "brings 'better, faster, smarter' efficiency to how marketers organize and collaborate, as well as how they reach and engage with consumers. In every way possible, Nestlé has strived to exploit the synergy of the two."

Three critical factors have helped Nestlé move closer to its digital leadership ambition. According to Pete, "They are relatively simple concepts, but the company has been diligent in their execution and delivery. They include: fundamentals remain fundamental; external focus and innovation; and rapid scaling and collaboration.

FUNDAMENTALS REMAIN FUNDAMENTAL

Nestlé has long-standing, fundamental convictions about the brand-building process based upon delighting consumers and enhancing lives. Digital and social media are not only fully compatible with these central principles, but help to accelerate and enhance the process.

Pete Blackshaw admits, "One of the things that attracted me to Nestlé was 'brand building the Nestlé way' (BBNW), the company's framework for building great brands. Within BBNW we talk about the fundamental requirements of 'creating engaging brand experiences', 'winning with shoppers' and 'knowing consumers deeply.' Within each we define more precisely the Nestlé way.

If one peels back the layers of digital vernacular, the fundamentals are already making a compelling case for digital acceleration. Consider Nestlé's approach to 'creating engaging brand experiences', where it is stressed that 'every consumer contact must be an attractive and rewarding brand experience'. One could argue that this is the perfect filter for figuring out a winning mobile strategy or a social media community management plan."

He cites Nestlé's Purina 2011 acquisition of Petfinder, the world's largest online pet adoption network. The site facilitates over 200,000 pet adoptions every year and users spend an average of six minutes on the site. "There is no question," he says, "that online content increases the experiential and engagement factor of the pet adoption process."

Another fundamental Nestlé belief is the significance of great copy and message quality. Pete also underscores that message quality— not media platform-- is the single biggest driver of brand and business impact. He emphasizes: "Industry debates about whether one or another social media platform works or does not work as an advertising vehicle largely miss the point. The more relevant question, and one Nestlé has been working relentlessly to address, is under what conditions each social media platform works best. Sales uplift, for instance, must be broken down into sequential requirements of reach, engagement (paying attention and viewing/reading) and of course action."

He adds, "Digital and social media pour new value into this equation through the power of amplification and sharing. If brands are successful with breakthrough copy, they generate positive 'earned media'. If they annoy, interrupt or distract with lower quality messaging, they get ignored, defriended or, worse, punished with negative 'spurned media,' all of which now can be measured with reasonably high levels of precision. Along the way, it is necessary to take specific steps to ensure that we are sufficiently prepared and 'ready' to amplify great content."

Pete Blackshaw is also quick to add a note of caution. "Brands frequently make the mistake of putting digital and certainly social media in a 'shiny new object silo.' It is sometimes treated as an exciting side-attraction to the marketing mix. While this may yield short-term gains and attention, it is frequently neither sustainable nor scalable."

Again, he emphasizes, "Fundamentals matter now more than ever."

EXTERNAL FOCUS AND INNOVATION

Pete describes how the second principle of Nestlé's digital transformation, external focus and innovation, takes several forms. Not only is the company invested in partnerships and collaboration with major consumer platforms like Facebook, Google, and Twitter, but it has established its own Silicon Valley Innovation Outpost.

Nestlé is committed to understanding how new platforms are disrupting consumer attention, creating engagement and providing brands with an opportunity to grow and evolve.

For example, Nestlé recently created Android KitKat, the latest version of the Android operating system, which reaches more than 1 billion devices. Google initiated the concept as an opportunity for joint synergies between the largest operating system and one of the world's favorite chocolate brands. Over 50 million Kit Kat bars featuring the Android logo were distributed across 17 markets, while also showcasing competitions to win new Nexus 7 devices and Google Play Store credits.

Nestlé is also working with Facebook to build unique relationship-building programs with its 210 million fans across 850 Nestlé Facebook pages. The foods giant is also taking advantage of tools like Google's Enterprise Analytics to gain richer insights from more than 1,000 Nestlé brand pages. Plus, Nestlé has embraced the fast-speed hackathon culture from major technology platforms and small start-ups to continually enhance their emphasis on external focus and innovation.

In addition, Nestlé has established a Silicon Valley Innovation Outpost to identify and apply breakthrough innovations quickly in the digital space. Pete believes, "By working more closely with established platforms as well as with high-potential start-ups, it is possible to understand consumers' needs better and respond to them more quickly."

Nestlé's outpost team has a clear focus on Nestlé's strategic priorities, especially around nutrition, health and wellness. "In fact," Pete adds, "the aim is to identify and leverage leading digital technology partners to delight consumers and enhance their health and wellness."

RAPID SCALING AND COLLABORATION

An idea that resulted from the company's first trip to Silicon Valley was the concept of bringing a slice of start-up culture to Nestlé's corporate headquarters in the form a Digital Acceleration Team (DAT). According to Pete, "This effort undergirds the third principle of digital transformation: rapid scaling and collaboration. The DAT was created as a new approach to foster speed, agility and digitally-powered brand building to Nestlé."

The initiative is comprised of Nestlé managers from around the world with digital brand-building competence, along with a rotation process to maximize learning through local market champions. The team works in the Vevey Consumer Engagement Center, a state-of-the-art facility that includes a multi-media content studio for creation and distribution of best practices. Team members manage social communities for global brands, address fast turn-around projects focused on digital or social media, and learn via an intensive training program anchored to the three pillars of Nestlé's digital strategy: listening, engaging and inspiring/transforming.

The overall concept has been so successful that it has already scaled to other major markets including India, China, Italy and Spain, with over a dozen others planned.

Pete elaborates, "The DAT in Nestlé's global headquarters works a bit like a venture capital firm. There is a large pipeline of business units and groups seeking DAT project time against an important need or opportunity. Based on the quality and seriousness of the pitch, DAT time will be allocated against that objective and very tight milestones and timing imperatives will be set for delivery. Over the past two years and four DAT classes, more than 100 projects have been delivered. Projects have included everything from how to improve digital recipe solutions to how to link the company's work in social responsibility (or what Nestlé terms 'creating shared value') with digital possibilities."

One very important DAT project helped lay the foundation for Nestlé's internal social media network, which has already made an impact on how the company collaborates and shares content. Through Salesforce.com's Chatter platforms— an internal version of Facebook with more specific corporate functionality — Nestlé hosts up to 200,000 employees and has created thousands of groups. Chatter is central to how the DAT team shares content and distributes how-to videos of value to brand builders.

"Just to put this in perspective," says Pete, "my own 'digital' sharing community has more than 3,000 users and nearly 80 per cent of the sharing comes from contributors in the markets. Many of Nestlé's top executives now use the platform to communicate in a more hands-on, high-touch manner. In many respects, social media represent an ideal 'operating principle' for a radically decentralized business network like Nestlé."

After discussing the three important building blocks —fundamentals, external focus and innovation and rapid scaling and collaboration —to Nestlé's digital strategy, Pete Blackshaw has some thoughts on leadership.

He says, "In the training I deliver to DAT leaders and digitally powered brand builders, I have no shortage of case studies, return on investment (ROI) frameworks and other guidance. But what I emphasize most is the importance of managing tension versus finding absolute answers. Digital realities in particular — from socialization to mobilization — put an urgent premium on understanding what I like to refer to as 'digital dualisms.' Dualisms are tension points or ostensible opposites. Classic digital dualisms include 'ROI versus intuition', 'formal versus informal power' and 'integration versus stimulation.'

The latter in particular is one all marketers (well beyond Nestlé) debate relentlessly. Should we have a stand-alone digital effort (stimulation) or should we ensure digital is included into all brand-building processes and guidance (integration)? The answer is that we need to straddle both to drive impact. The degree to which one dials up or down depends on the environmental context."

Without question, Pete Blackshaw understands what it takes to leverage a digital transformation to build brands and delight consumers, and in the process, he has also led a company and an industry through both his experience and his inspiration.

Pete Blackshaw's background is nothing short of motivational.

He was named an **Internationalist of the Year** *in 2011. Prior to his position at Nestlé, he served as Chief Marketing Officer of NM Incite, the collaboration between Nielsen and consulting firm McKinsey, created to improve businesses performance by realizing social media intelligence and consumer insights.*

The Nielsen/McKinsey role was the culmination of Pete's entrepreneurial years.

He founded PlanetFeedback.com in 1999 as an Internet portal focused on consumer feedback. Three years later, Planetfeedback was acquired by Cincinnati-based marketing intelligence firm Intelliseek, where Pete served as Chief Marketing & Customer Satisfaction Officer. During this time, he also co-founded the Word-of-Mouth Marketing Association (WOMMA), and continues to serve on its board. Intelliseek was acquired by BuzzMetrics in 2006.

Nielsen then purchased both NetRatings and BuzzMetrics in 2007, and combined the two companies to form Nielsen Online. Pete served as CMO of BuzzMetrics, which helps companies better understand the power of online consumers who share experiences, advice, opinions on topics ranging from customer service to product performance. Today, BuzzMetrics is part of NM Incite.

A Harvard Business School grad, his initial marketing training, though, was at Procter & Gamble as a brand manager in the paper sector. However, the online impetus appeared even then—the mid '90s. He helped co-found P&G first interactive marketing unit with early initiatives like online sampling and online advertising qualification.

He's also given back to his Cincinnati home. Pete contributed to establishing Cincinnati as a consumer marketing "Hub of Innovation" with a state designation that provided $250,000 in seed money to promote the industry's growth.

Amy Lou

of Huawei Discusses how Building an Ecosystem Challenges Marketers to Embrace Transformation

Amy Lou
Director of Global Brand Management
Huawei
Shenzen, China & London,
United Kingdom

FAST FACTS
Where were you born?
China, but now live in London. As an
"in-betweener" culturally, I've developed rich insights about markets,
consumers and the way of marketing
in both Asia and Europe by having
worked, traveled and lived in both
regions.

*Was there a lesson you learned in an
early first job that still applies now?*
A lesson I learned when I start to work for Huawei is very beneficial to a marketer:
• Logic (Everything you do, have a clear thinking pattern, even for creative. There has
  to be clear logic.)
• Data (Use data to generate insights, not subjective opinion.)
• Benchmark (Need to understand the competitive environment and understand
  what others are doing. Not just in one's category, but benchmark the best out
  there. You will then be able to provide a constructive viewpoint.)

What is the best advice you were ever given?
Inspired by the motto from Peking University where I studied my bachelor degree:
"Be independently-minded. Embrace the diversity."

What was your big career break?
(Or at least the one you learned the most from!) I learned this lesson from a global
brand campaign I developed: For a product-driven category, a product campaign
should focus on telling a resonating product story and demonstrating how to fits
into people's lives. It has the different role compared to a brand campaign. For a
new product launch, it is not sufficient to convey a proposition via a slogan.

What's your favorite city for business travel?
If I have to pick up one city I like the most in Europe outside London, it will be Barcelona. It is a Mediterranean city filled with passion and art. Plus it has sea, sunshine, and delicious food. A city you can do business in a feel less uptight.

What's your favorite place in the world?
London remains my favourite place to live in the world. It is a city with a rich history, a diversified culture and a fascinating art scene; It's a city that never stops inspiring and always catches you with its dry humor.

WITHOUT QUESTION, AMY LOU BELIEVES THAT THE FUTURE OF MARKETING IS ABOUT BUILDING AN ECOSYSTEM, not campaigns. Her experience of working to establish that ecosystem at Huawei, the world's largest telecommunications equipment maker, underscores that she understands how this process challenges marketers to change established mind-sets and embrace transformation.

Over the past 25 years, the company has established three core values: 1. Consumer-centric focus, 2. Dedication, and 3. Innovation. According to Amy Lou, "The commitment of continuous investment in innovation is the key success factor at Huawei. In fact, Huawei invested USD 5.1B in R&D in 2013 alone. We are confronted with an increasing amount of content, applications, devices, and interaction among people. It is overwhelming. Users demand better experiences, such as simplicity, speed, and smart sharing. This demand is the force that drives the ICT industry forward."

Huawei has 3 different business groups with the corporation-- Carrier Business, Enterprise Business and Consumer Business. In the smartphone market, Huawei started as an ODM (Original Design Manufacturer), cooperating with top global operators to develop feature phones. Huawei Device officially became Huawei Consumer BG in 2011, and started its transformation from a respected B2B company to a new, rapidly-embraced B2C brand.

Amy's role as Director of Global Brand Management is a daunting one; however, her dedication to the advancement of contemporary marketing values insures that she's up to the task. Her belief is that marketing innovation in our Digital/Social Age means "braving the power of difference." She elaborates: "Humans are attracted to difference. Our brain encodes difference more forcefully. Difference awakens sensation and creates enduring memories. Today, difference is even more important. Difference catches attention, triggers curiosity, and boosts the conversation. Marketers should be courageous enough to think out of box, break industry norms, challenge established conventions, and embrace the power of difference. Ultimately this drives innovation in marketing, but it also creates successful brands and strong consumer connections."

As a result, she suggests that contemporary marketers might consider the following new values she's adopted at Huawei:

- Champion a total ecosystem solution, instead of considering ideas for individual disciplines like PR, advertising, digital or social.
- Unleash the power of owned media to make an ALWAYS ON ENGAGEMENT PLATFORM to tell a brand story and convey a brand voice.
- Inspire "trans-boundary" ideas and initiatives to drive innovation in marketing. Brave the disruptive ideas. Create new rules of the game.

Amy Lou accepts that as art is the reflection of an era, marketing similarly captures cultural and social trends. Today, though, that culture is also shaped by consumer interaction.

"In the past decade," she says, "we have seen the fundamental shift in how marketers engage with consumers. The continuous emergence of new technologies has drastically affected our lifestyle and changed consumer behavior. Ubiquitous internet, emergence of social media and penetration of smartphones have extensively changed the way we live in 21st century. The most significant change in marketing today is consumer behavior. Humans shape technology. Technology changes human behavior. Human behavior influences the way we do marketing."

The two transformative factors in consumer behavior are the actions of being always on and multi-screen. Smart devices have become both immersive and inseparable in a consumer's life. A phone is the last thing someone puts away before bed and the first thing they reach for upon waking. Throughout the day, people constantly check their device—from posting a selfie on FB, chatting on WeChat or WhatsApp, playing a game, reading a newspaper, to booking a flight, reserving a restaurant, or reordering dog food. Consumers are always on. This presents challenges to brands. Engaging with ALWAYS ON requires a new definition of a brand's role so that it fits into a consumer's life.

Multi-screen is another dimension of digitalized consumer behavior. Or as Amy likes to say, "You screen. I screen. We are all screen." Multi-screen is the new norm as indicted by IDG research (May 2014):

- 87% of people is using tablets while watching TV;
- 51% of people is using smartphone while watching TV;
- 50% of users read newspaper on tablet, 41% on smartphone;

She recognizes that ALWAYS ON and MULTI SCREEN consumer behavior also requires an ecosystem that is similarly ALWAYS ON, as well as HOLISTIC. For Amy, this means developing an ALWAYS ON PLATFORM to enable constant engagement with an audience via a well-planned content strategy that requires great time, effort and care. It also means developing a TRULY INTEGRATED SOLUTION to amplify the communications idea among paid, owned and earned media. She adds, "The needs of a consumer's multi-screen behavior should be addressed in the solution. It requires strong leadership to champion integration within the organization."

The nature of ALWAYS ON and MULTI SCREEN behavior has dramatically changed the media landscape. For Amy, reaching and engaging with consumers is no longer a linear process. She says, "The traditional communications funnel model that moves from awareness, familiarity, preference to purchase and recommendation is no longer relevant in this digital age. The media landscape is ever evolving, almost beyond recognition compared to what it was a decade ago. How to reach and engage with the digitalized audiences is the driver behind the changes in marketing today."

The biggest change she's seen in her career is how marketing is shifting from the dominance of paid media to the integration of paid, owned and earned media. "Paid media is just part of the equation; in fact, it is gradually diminishing in dominance. Instead owned media is becoming a pivotal platform to tell a compelling story and effectively engage with audiences. Earned media now serves to build fame around a brand swiftly to boost awareness, as well as affinity."

She had developed a number of key marketing principles to help brands navigate amid the transformation occurring today:

· Principle #1: Audiences First

Understanding always on and multi-screen audiences, and grasp deep insights of their 24/7 lifestyle. Identify the passion points and contemporary culture tensions that may feed into compelling, resonant storytelling.

Map out your consumer's purchase journey and identify the key touch points at each stage of the journey. Understand what they are looking for at those VERY MOMENTS and develop a relevant content strategy. This is now the new notion of TARGETED COMMUNICATIONS. Give consumers what they need at precisely the RIGHT MOMENT.

Go beyond target audience to identify influencers. Provide influencers with the fuel to ignite buzz, so an instant hit online becomes feasible.

· Principle #2: Winning Content Strategy

An average TVC with massive media spend can still achieve reach for a campaign. However, in this digital age when a brand must earn the right for people to share and evangelize, average is not the winning formula.

Content strategy must be coherent and compelling. This means relevant, entertaining, original and engaging. The DancePonyDance commercial from Three, a mobile phone operator, achieved 4 million YouTube views within a week of hitting the screens. The pony featured in the commercial has become a celebrity through viewer sharing. It never failed bringing a smile to people's face.

As a marketer, there is often a judgment call to be made when determining the fine balance of staying on brand and being bold enough to be "edgy" or different.

· Principle #3: Become topical

Being topical requires out-of-the-box thinking to trigger a viral effect, yet brand authenticity cannot be lost in the process. The recent buzz around the Ice bucket competition of ALS (Amyotrophic Lateral Sclerosis) is a typical case of out-of-the-box thinking in leveraging the power of social media to make it an instant hit online. The reasons behind the online sensation are:

1) Leveraging the nature of 24/7 social media age (being entertaining);

2) Showcasing the power of celebrity (leverage endorsement);

3 Understanding deep insights about human nature (response to challenges as the motivation to participate);

4) Setting a meaningful purpose (compelling story-telling).

Over the past eight years, Amy Lou has been in the rare position of building international brands from their earliest beginnings for two Asia-based technology companies. Prior to Huawei, headquartered in Shenzhen, China, she served as Head of Brand and Marketing Communications for HTC Corporation, the Taiwanese manufacturer of smart-phones and tablets. It was for this role that she was named a 2007 **Internationalist of the Year**.

Given today's obvious interest in China, her experiences are of tremendous value to other globally-minded marketers. She predictably has strong opinions about the future of Chinese international brands, as well as clear recommendations for marketing brands from China around the world. And, most importantly, she's a realist.

According to Amy Lou, "Among the 2013 Interbrand Top 100 Brands list, 55 brands are from Unites States. China, as the world's second economy, hasn't got a single brand on the list. It is the fact today, but it will not be the fact for the years to come. Chinese companies are going international. An article from The Guardian (Jun 3, 2014) titled "Chinese technology companies poised to dominate the world" has predicted the era of Chinese brands going global with companies like Lenovo, Huawei, Tencent, Baidu, ZTE, and Alibaba topping the list.

She admits that building a Chinese international brand is challenging, and she name three current obstacles:

1) A shortage of talent that has knowledge of the Chinese market and culture, and also possesses global brand development and management expertise.

2) Chinese companies have a strong organization culture combined with Chinese way of doing business. Adapting to the organizational culture is a huge challenge for an outsider. Language is the obvious barrier for any foreigner who hopes to dive into the business as quickly as possible. Hindered communications will affect the quality of decisions.

3) Chinese products are currently perceived as being inexpensive and of low quality. There have also been issues of "trustworthiness" in the West. This is a burden to all those Chinese companies who have the ambition to go international.

Despite all the challenges listed above, the trend for Chinese brands to expand internationally is irreversible. A marketer may need to be a pioneer, but also should develop knowledge about Chinese culture, understand the Chinese way of doing business, and have deep insights about the market and consumers in both China and other markets of the world. She adds, "Equally important is that a marketer have an international perspective to marry the best of the East and the West. Bilingual ability will be a big plus to take on this challenge."

According to Amy, a pioneer herself, there is no proven winning formula for taking a Chinese brand global. However, she does share a few key principles derived from her experience and observations thus far:

Principle #1: Dial up the best of brand heritage and tap into the universal human truth

Be authentic! Stay truthful to the DNA of a brand and define a purposeful positioning based on company ethos and enduring human truth.

This also means respecting the brand roots and bringing the best of this heritage to the world. In the eyes of many, China embodies a new energy and hope, and represents a powerful new dream for a bright future—despite its issues and problems. China also has a widely-recognized legacy in art and culture. A Chinese brand should consider leveraging this familiarity, yet also strive to create a brand offering with a refreshing point of view about the category. It empowers the brand to be different, memorable and topical.

Principle # 2: Build personality. Leverage humor.

On a world stage, one of the vital qualities for a leader is charisma. A strong brand needs to demonstrate a charismatic personality, not just the image a faceless company.

Being modest is a highly-appreciated virtue in China. People have been educated to be modest and not stand out from the crowd. Clearly this rule doesn't apply to brand building in the 21st century. Chinese brands need to be bold and brave to showcase their distinctive brand personality and create a reason to generate brand love. Of course, that brand personality should be credible and reflect the image and values of the company. Everyone within the organization should behave as the brand personality dictates.

On the world stage, the Chinese have the perception of being a serious people. The truth is that the Chinese love humor and have their own interpretation of humor. To engage with the western audiences, humor can be a powerful tool. Despite the difference between the appreciation of humor in the West and China, there are some universal underlying principles. Entertainment has become important in today's efforts to drive earned media. This is the territory marketers should examine to create a refreshing Chinese brand with a great sense of humor.

Principle #3: Relentlessly create a premium image with craftsmanship in every detail

As China shifts from low-end, labor-intensive manufacturing to high-end, technology-driven manufacturing, its brand perceptions will ultimately change.

Creating a premium image, however, is a vital part of taking Chinese brand global. Not only does this apply to products and services, but to everything related to delivering excellent brand experiences across all consumers' touch points—including packaging, website, advertising, retail environment and after-sale services. Apple is great benchmark in delivering premium brand experience and driving quality in every single detail of brand experience. Chinese brands should relentlessly pursue quality. As a marketer must also be an internal champion to advocate the notion of quality and be its best guardian of the brand image—from look, feel, voice, to behavior.

On the subject of Chinese brands, she also likes to add, "Each country has its national trait. Germany is famous for its superior engineering. Japan is well-known for the excellence of quality management. The United States is reputable about being innovative. Scandinavian is appreciated in design.

In today's social world, consumers can access to all kinds of reviews to examine the quality and user experience of a product. These reviews give consumers a reference when comparing products from different makers. The familiarity of a brand, the endorsement from influencers, and positive WOM all contribute to providing confidence to consumers at the time of purchase.

When consumers purchase a product, the national trait is an integral part of decision making. But the impact of national traits embedded in the country of origin have become very subtle in light of all these other performance considerations of greater interest to today's consumers."

So what is the future of telecommunications, according to Huawei?

Amy Lou has an immediate answer: "At Huawei, we believe the future will be a connected world with infinite possibilities. We are committed to building a more efficient and integrated information logistics system linking people to people, people to things, and things to things. We are connecting systems, businesses, cities, societies and people around the globe, improving efficiencies, transforming industries, creating better experiences for everyone and enabling free exchanges of thoughts and ideas."

Amy Lou is a Global Brand Management Director with in-depth experience of both European and Asian markets having worked, traveled and lived in both territories. Her key expertise lies in developing and nurturing brands through the assessment rigor of the marketplace, while also developing insightful strategy to propel companies forward. Combined with strong creative instincts and years of experience in brand communications, she has consistently delivered business growth as well as brand metric advances.

Currently Ms. Lou is Global Brand Management Director of Consumer BG at Huawei, where she is responsible for developing brand architecture to transform Huawei into a strong consumer brand that is embraced worldwide. She manages all global brand strategy and planning, as well as consumer-facing communications.

Prior to her role at Huawei, she was Head of Brand and Marketing Communications for HTC Europe Ltd from 2006 to 2011. As one of the marketing pioneers at HTC, Amy helped to successfully transform HTC into a globally-acknowledged brand, ranked in the top 100 global brands by Interbrand in October 2011.

Amy Lou began her career at Motorola China in 1994, as a Senior Marketing Manager where she was responsible for marketing communications within Motorola's mobile business. During her eight years at Motorola, she led awarding-winning campaigns and also worked within the branding team at Motorola US as a job rotation.

Amy Lou was named an **Internationalist of the Year** *in 2007 and one of the "Top 100 Leaders by Internationalist" in 2011 and 2014.*

Barbara Basney

Talks about the Global Transformation of a Legacy Brand

Barbara Basney

Vice President Global Advertising & Media

Xerox Corporation

Norwalk, Connecticut USA

FAST FACTS

Where were you born?
New Jersey. Grew up in Germany.

Was there a lesson you learned in an early first job that still applies now?
You will never feel 100% ready when an opportunity arises — so embrace the apprehension and forge ahead.

What is the best advice you were ever given?
Failure will be a better teacher than success.

What's your favorite city for business travel?
Paris

What's your favorite place in the world?
Atop a Tepui in Venezuela

BARBARA BASNEY IN HER ROLE AS VICE PRES-
IDENT OF GLOBAL ADVERTISING and Media has
been at the forefront of an extraordinary evolution of
the Xerox Corporation as the world-renown company
has transformed from its heritage in document technology to the leading enterprise for business processes services throughout the globe. Over the past several years, she has not only worked to communicate the
significance of this transition for so iconic a brand, but
has also embraced new ways of advertising. She acknowledges how real-time operational integration and
new thoughts about content are shifting the way she
approaches both her work and her role within one of
the world's iconic global organizations.

Barbara admits that Xerox has undertaken a "massive transformation." Today, more than half of the company's revenues come from
business processes or "back office solutions and services" for companies, governments and municipalities around the world-- in areas like
Human Resources, Customer Care, Healthcare, Public Transportation,
and Finance and Accounting.   The company is helping "behind the
scenes" to simplify how work gets done-- whether collecting 37 billion
public transit fares annually, handling 1.6 million customer care interactions daily, processing 900 million health insurance claims every year, or
handling $421 billion in accounts payables per annum.

The idea of conveying just what today's Xerox does for customers
is at the core of Barbara's role, and campaigns like "Made Simple by
Xerox" and "Ready for Real Business" have reshaped how customers in
over 180 countries-- from small businesses to large global enterprises–

perceive the brand. Barbara says, "There are many ways that we're help-ing our customers around the world simplify the way work gets done, so they can focus on what really matters—their real business."

She adds, "From the company's inception and Chester Carlson's invention of xerography, Xerox was never just about creating copies, but always about simplifying how work gets done. So making things easier, as well as more efficient and more productive has always been part of our company ethos."

The story of Xerox's corporate transformation is extraordinary given how the company started with an enviable 100% brand awareness among senior-level executives before the 2010 acquisition of ACS, which formed the basis of its new services division. Of course, that perfect brand awareness score was linked to the company's document and print-ing heritage, so Xerox had the new challenge of repositioning itself as a company *also* recognized for business process services, without sacri-ficing its legacy and reputation. Then, to add urgency to so significant a task, the new business services sector was also considered critical to Xerox's future growth. Just as the company had once made duplicating information as simple as pushing a button, Xerox now needed the world to know it could simplify a wide range of back-office business tasks for their customers.

In 2010, Barbara and her team started by launching a repositioning campaign centered on building credibility and trust in their new busi-ness process services. This was executed by using customer testimonials from well-respected companies like Procter & Gamble, Michelin, Target, Ducati and Marriott to convey how these leaders relied on Xerox for their outsourced services.

While the approach successfully highlighted their customers, Xerox felt it needed a second phase of communications to refocus on its own core story. Interestingly, the initial insight remained the same– simplify how work gets done. The difference, though, was to tell the Xerox story using facts and numbers to powerfully convey the scale and scope of the company's business services. This phase introduced RealBusiness.com as a destination to present the new Xerox and provide "small nuggets" of relevant content for an extremely busy C-Suite/Senior Executive audience. A social media aggregator was built into the site to display current news and conversations in the Services space, while other content marketing projects beyond the website helped to increase the impact of Xerox as a thought leader in the category.

Integral to the success of a program like "Business Made Simple by Xerox" is content, and Barbara Basney is the first to acknowledge that today's advertising environment, more than ever before, lends itself to the use of content to create essential conversations with key brand audiences. "It's a super powerful tool," she says, "as it provides a great opportunity for relevant storytelling, which is so critical to expressing a brand voice today."

However, she also admits, "At Xerox, we are trying to be very careful with a platform like Real Business to only present content on topics with which we'd like align our brand—rather than talk just about us. True thought leadership provides something of interest to a key audience segment. A vignette or piece of information can also attract attention, because it is unexpected. We want people to be pleased or intrigued that a memorable element of content was brought to them by Xerox. It demonstrates that we care about our audience. And in today's 'sharing environment,' it doesn't hurt when someone passes on something we provide them, or other media pick up some of these articles."

She continues: "Chest-beating is easy for brands—it's largely been our history. Inviting someone in is difficult. Finding an angle that is interesting and thought-provoking enough for a person to internalize or attentively consider is far more powerful than any straight-forward message."

Barbara Basney can talk at length about the evolution of content creation, how it affects her thinking about paid, earned and owned media, as well as her experimentation with new content platforms—including variations of native advertising, sponsored opportunities, and what she terms as "the many shades of grey" surrounding content and advertising-- or an area that she reminds us was defined as "church and state" not so long ago. Still, she recognizes that the essential benefit of any content play is to insure that it adds benefit to an audience eager to consume information relevant to their needs.

Native advertising does play a role in Xerox's marketing mix. Yet, Barbara also notes paradoxically, "The opportunity of native advertising is also its challenge." She believes it is difficult to create content that seamlessly integrates with a publisher's brand, while also factoring in how the native environment should optimally align with an advertiser's message. In other words, the process can be tricky at best. "It's hard to execute equally well for both the advertiser and the publisher," she says.

Yet, Xerox has been quite innovative and successful in its use of native advertising, or integrating its marketing content with a third-party website. Barbara admits that a number of initiatives have helped to change perceptions and further the repositioning of the Xerox brand.

In addition to the complexity of finding the right native advertising alignment for both the advertiser and publisher, she points out other issues she's now come to recognize. In fact, Barbara can't emphasize enough how most advertisers tend to do too much "chest beating" with content. "This really doesn't work well as a native program on a publisher's site, especially when existing corporate content, like sales and marketing material, is repurposed."

Her advice is to substantially edit any company-generated content to be sure it meets standards of quality and relevance, and is also appropriate and respectful of both the advertiser's brand and the publisher's site. She stresses, "It all needs to work together to tell a story."

She also advocates creating rules for rigorous content creation standards. "Too often, the content a brand wants to share is not of great interest to the audience, or it appears too much like marketing material. Always consider quality and relevance."

Another issue she acknowledges is measurement. "Advertisers," she warns, "have to become more comfortable with the ambiguity and looser metrics associated with native advertising programs. We now expect hard metrics from digital initiatives. However, because native advertising opportunities are typically customized programs, they are rarely directly comparable, and the available measureable elements of each program can vary widely. The more programs we implement, the more we grow our internal repository of some 'directional' metrics, but the lack of KPIs is a downside."

As a result, she suggests that a portion of a budget should be set aside to "test and learn" in today's fast-changing content landscape. "At Xerox, we've made it a point to try a variety of approaches with native and content-based initiatives with different publishers. Being diversified and exploratory lets us leverage the audiences of our publishing partners."

In addition to the significance of content, one of the biggest changes Barbara has experienced in marketing today is the need for real-time operational integration. "In the past, the marketing department was organized by function—advertising, public relations, sponsorships, digital. Although we'd certainly share information, we essentially operated independently. Today that's simply not possible as too many of our functions and missions overlap."

She explains that true operational integration needs to occur as "we are all activating together now to take advantage of such fast-flowing market opportunities. Even 'silos' of paid, earned, owned, and shared are just nomenclature, and maximizing their integration should be top of mind. For that reason, functional teams within a company must work closely on an almost real-time basis to operationalize these opportunities and get the full value of the benefit. his kind of inter-department integration really does prove how the sum, or results, is so much greater than the parts."

The next step will be for Xerox to integrate their agency partners into this process. As a centrally-focused global brand, Xerox uses a total of ten specialist agencies in key marketing functions from content creation, brand initiatives, sponsorship, PR, to creative, media, digital and other disciplines. Although that may be fewer agencies than many other sprawling multinationals, Barbara admits that their roster has gotten bigger in light of the company's needs in a dramatically changing marketplace.

Again, she underscores that real-time operational integration is more than structure, it is also process. "It changes how we think about every business function-- from who's invited to a meeting to seeing opportunities and creating ideas that wouldn't have occurred when everyone was sitting alone in silos." Xerox is also exploring how such integration will work on a global level. Barbara notes that currently the US is at the forefront of this change. "Many roles and traditional definitions are being turned upside down every day—right now, more in the US than elsewhere. It is a very big shift."

Big shifts, though, are becoming her specialty, so there's little doubt that such change can only be positive. When Barbara Basney looks ahead—even as marketing is in tremendous transition—she believes that the future is simply filled with new possibilities as the evolution of technology, media and messaging continue.

Barbara is responsible for Xerox brand and product advertising in more than 35 countries, including traditional television, print, radio and outdoor, as well as digital media. Her responsibilities include the formulation of advertising strategies, campaign development and implementation, and media mix optimization, with a focus on integrating and amplifying paid, owned and earned media.

Barbara joined Xerox in 2000 as a director of marketing communications for the Office Printing Division located in Portland, Ore. Prior to joining Xerox, she spent more than 15 years in marketing and advertising for both B-to-B and B-to-C Fortune 100 corporations including Rite-Aid, Tektronix and Convergys. Basney has managed functions including advertising, public relations, corporate communications, direct marketing, tradeshows, customer communications and marketing strategy.

She is a Board Member of the Ad Council and the International Advertising Association, active in the Association of National Advertisers (ANA) the Advertising Women of New York, and the National Advertising Review Board. Barbara was named an **Internationalist of the Year** in 2011. She is on the Annual List of 100 Marketing Leaders by The Internationalist, and has been named by Brand Innovators as one of the top 50 women in brand marketing.

A Cherry Hill, N.J. native, she grew up in Germany. She received a bachelor's degree in business administration from the College of William and Mary in Williamsburg, Va. and a master's degree in business administration from Portland State University in Portland, Oregon. She currently resides in Stamford, Connecticut.

CHALLENGING
the Status Quo
to Create
New Frameworks

Simon Sproule

Builds Tesla's Global Image in a New World by Challenging Classic Marketing Concepts

Simon Sproule

Corporate Vice President of Global Communications
Tesla Motors
Palo Alto, California USA

FAST FACTS
Where were you born?
Basingstoke, UK

Was there a lesson you learned in an early first job that still applies now?
Being able to get out of bed early and get ahead of the day. Lesson learned while being a student and doing vacation jobs.

What is the best advice you were ever given?
Build a career in an industry that you are personally interested in.

What was your big career break?
Being posted to Japan to take up the role of Global Communications VP at Nissan

Are you willing to admit your biggest career mistake? (Or at least the one you learned the most from!)
I wish I had pushed faster for the integration of marketing and communications throughout my career.

Where do you turn for inspiration?
My family.

What's your favorite city for business travel?
New York

What's your favorite place in the world?
Provence, France

THERE IS NO QUESTION THAT TESLA IS REVOLU-
TIONIZING THE AUTOMOTIVE INDUSTRY. A company created by contemporary Renaissance Man Elon
Musk, Tesla builds highly-desirable, elegant, heart-rac-
ing electric cars that are completely compatible with
starring as champions for the environment. Plus, the
company is taking bold risks to entirely disrupt a
long-established automobile sales structure. Indisput-
ably, the brand is at the crosshairs of technology and
the advancement of personal transportation. So why
wouldn't its approach to marketing also challenge classic ideals, as well as overturning tried-and-true notions
about what sells cars?

Simon Sproule, who joined Tesla earlier this year as the company's
Corporate Vice President of Global Communications, has spent his
career in automotive marketing and communications by breaking down
silos and embracing sprawling global programs with discipline, clarity
and collaboration. He is an outspoken advocate for the integration of
marketing and communications, and has achieved a number of critical
milestones while in roles for The Nissan Motor Company in Yokohama
and The Renault-Nissan Alliance in Paris.

In other words, there couldn't be a better marriage between a
brand and its marketing champion. Yet, as an Englishman, he humbly
discusses Tesla as "a small company with an outsized level of interest
and reputation." Don't for a minute, though, underestimate his ambi-
tions for the brand. They are enormous.

Tesla's ultimate goal is to encourage everyone to drive electric
cars. Simon cites an industry projection of 100 million cars on roads

throughout the world by 2020, and Tesla's plan is to accelerate that transition. He says, "How society approaches personal mobility is changing—from Uber to Zip Cars to new means of auto sharing, as well as evolving views of how people want to live and what they want to drive. It's not a question of will electric cars be around, it is simply a matter of adoption rate and how fast this will grow over time. The mission of Tesla is to make electric cars viable for everyone."

Given Tesla's current reputation and price tag, that democratic ideal may raise a few eyebrows; however, the company chose to enter the high-end of the business first. The SUV / Crossover is launching next year (2015) and the smaller car around three years from now (2017). Simon also expects that by their debut, electric cars will be more widespread as other manufacturers enter the business, creating a tipping point for both price and recharging infrastructure to insure that consumers need not compromise with a gas-powered vehicle for fear of running out of electricity.

He admits that Tesla is young, bold and ambitious. Many of the brand's early adopters love technology, care about the environment, and just happen to be either famous or wealthy. One sees plenty of Tesla's P85 Model S in Silicon Valley and throughout the greater New York City area where the car is immediately recognized and admired. This certainly helps the company scale up its reputation and aware-ness. He adds, "Now, though, the brand is also becoming desirable to a broader demographic that may want to reduce their carbon load, but also get on with their daily lives. Tesla is in their consideration set."

Again, though, Simon Sproule emphasizes that Tesla may have started as a premium and aspirational vehicle, but the company's vision is clear—it will provide electric cars for as many people as possible in as many places as possible. He also cites statistics on global automobile growth as hundreds of millions of people will have increasing needs for personal mobility. "China," he says, "may be the world's largest car market, but the number of cars per thousand is quite low at 50, compared with the US, for example, where car ownership is at 800 per every thousand people. Also, as more Chinese migrate to cities, the challenges with pollution and traffic continue. Already there are less restrictions for low and zero emission vehicles. There's no question that the automobile industry is anticipating global growth."

So what is Tesla's marketing and communications strategy?

According to Simon, "It's certainly very non-traditional. We don't advertise. There are no paid endorsements. We don't buy media. Everyone who purchases the car pays the same price. Yet we are using a number of contemporary strategies on a mass level."

He continues: "It is experiencing the product that is convincing. People simply drive it and love it. We gain exposure and awareness through physical events, so people can see, touch and experience the cars. And then we invest heavily in content. Today people have a broad range of distinct ways in which they consume content and interact with media. We believe in storytelling through our own channels, so that our potential customers can view our content in their own time. We work to insure that it adds some value to their lives, and is compelling enough to share."

There's no question that Simon Sproule sees contemporary content strategies as central to marketing effectiveness today. He says, "Great brands must have a powerful content strategy as the backbone of their marketing communications. A brand is a story. Not only is the story the mainstay of the product, but it provides both the lure and the combination of one's experiences with the brand."

He adds, "Breakthrough brands today—whether Red Bull, Burberry or GoPro-- are increasingly from organizations that have transformed themselves into content companies. In a world where advertising can easily be blocked or avoided, every brand in the world is trying to figure out how to reach people and tell their stories. How else do we introduce Tesla to those who don't know the brand, understand it, or even have an interest in electric cars? As a result, some of the best brands are effectively media companies now."

Simon's passion for the company insures that he tells Tesla's most compelling story—for now and the future. "In any business," he says, "you have to strike a balance between achieving short-term profit and sales commitments, while at the same time, build the image of the brand to keep the upper parts of the purchase funnel full of interested consumers. If you look at the world's most valuable brands, they achieve a very good balance between communicating the immediate benefits of their products or services, and telling consumers why the brand or company should be trusted for the long term."

Simon Sproule does not doubt that for Tesla to succeed, it needs strong marketing. He believes, however, that we are experiencing a marketing communications evolution where terms like "above the line" and "below the line" no longer matter. The arbitrary "line" has dissolved, and true marketing communications integration is critical.

Since his days at Nissan, he has been a vocal advocate that "the future of the industry is full integration." While in Japan, Simon spent several years insuring that Nissan's marketing and communications divisions functioned seamlessly as one unit. He fostered a program of worldwide collaboration to accelerate Nissan's brand power in support of the company's expansive business plan, and also launched the first global brand campaign in the company's history. Plus, he was a champion for combining two key functions: Integrated Brand Communications and Global Corporate Communications. He can demonstrate how the combination of the two disciplines benefited the Japanese auto giant through greater flexibility across platforms.

Now he adds that "Integration is also about content. Today, many marketers are overly obsessed about the channel. However, channels are ideally co-owned by both the marketing and public relations disciplines. They must be in sync. Social media has pushed this alignment, and success is increasingly defined as content driven, and based on what people choose to consume."

Today's new challenge for content creators, though, is how do you inform and entertain people, and through which platforms? Simon muses, "Marketing and creative people often find themselves in a tough place when they have to justify how a 30: spot contributes to a consumer's day. I'm not saying that traditional creative, media, and advertising doesn't work. These industries will be around for a very long time. And there's no question that after a series of sustained messages, sales will follow. But not everyone is able to convince the CFO that allocating another $100 million in creative and media will definitely move the sales needle."

Interestingly, while Simon was at Nissan, the launch of the GT-R supercar underscored another benefit to combined communications departments. The launch was carried out solely through PR, word of mouth and interactive. Such a radically different media mix was a first for Nissan anywhere in the world, and orders for the car in Japan sold out rapidly.

Right now, Tesla's channel selection excludes paid media, and instead focuses on events, public relations, social media, and content. Simon does think regularly about whether he can build sufficient awareness and demand without paid media. Nonetheless, he joined Tesla, a company he believes in, to test that he can build a strong global brand and generate increased sales with an entirely different, non-traditional marketing communications approach. (And we have no doubt that Simon Sproule can do just that.)

Simon Sproule is a true internationalist with over 20 years of auto industry experience. He began his career at Ford UK, and in 1998 moved to Ford's global operations in Dearborn, Michigan. Shortly thereafter, he assumed the North American communications lead for Jaguar. Aston Martin and Land Rover were added to his responsibilities in 2001.

In 2003, he joined Nissan North America as the Vice President of Communications, moving to the company's headquarters in Tokyo the following year. His role eventually expanded to CVP of global marketing communications at Nissan Motor Company and director of marketing communications for the Renault-Nissan Alliance. He was named an **Internationalist of the Year** *in 2007.*

Simon was born and raised in the UK and has a Geography degree from London University, which he claims helps with his international life. He has lived in all the world's cities that are associated with marketing or with cars: London, Detroit, New York, Los Angeles, Tokyo, Paris and now San Francisco.

As of November 1, 2014, Simon has decided to accept a new challenge. He is joining Aston Martin as their new Head of Marketing and Communications, and will be moving back to the UK after 17 years.

Clayton Ruebensaal

of the
The Ritz-Carlton
Envisions a New Era
of Brand
Communications

Clayton Ruebensaal
Vice President Global Marketing
The Ritz-Carlton Hotel Company
Chevy Chase, Maryland USA

FAST FACTS
Where were you born?
Washington DC

Was there a lesson you learned in an early first job that still applies now?
Love what you do. If you don't, keep looking because everyone deserves to love their work.

What is the best advice you were ever given?
Work hard

Are you willing to admit your biggest career mistake? (Or at least the one you learned the most from!)
My biggest mistake was jumping too quickly at a huge job before asking the basic questions that anyone with more wisdom would have.

Where do you turn for inspiration?
I'm inspired by the brilliance and competitiveness in Silicon Valley. Visually, I'm inspired by architecture and photography, so I spend a lot of time in museums.

What's your favorite city for business travel?
Tokyo. The speed, the attention to detail, and the culture of excellence make you bring your A game.

What's your favorite place in the world?
Thailand. I grew up there and always ache to return.

CLAYTON RUEBENSAAL IS NOT SHY about voicing an opinion on a heady subject like the future of marketing.

"If this is the age of consumer control," he says, "next will come an age of brand control." A provocative statement at a time when many marketers are accepting consumers as content co-creators who can influence a brand's voice, if not its future direction. However, Clayton, at heart, is a marketing purist, even as he embraces the new, and as Vice President Global Marketing of Ritz-Carlton Hotels, both current and future concepts of brand communications have been at the center of his thoughts since accepting the role in 2010. And he has delivered on both revolutionary work and breakthrough results for the company, to boot.

He continues, "Brands will come out of this era unsatisfied with the result of where consumers have taken their brands, and realize they need to take a much more proactive role in managing the communications about their brands. It's not to say consumers can't co-create, but that brands need to have the vision and the plan to lead that conversation. Even in the world of social media, I believe brands will shape or orchestrate messages more in the future than they do today. It's too common for brands to say they are being reactive, because they put consumers first. It doesn't have to be either or. You can put consumers first still have a plan for the conversation you'll be having with them. Not doing so would be like having a dinner party without a menu or schedule of events, because you respect your guests so much that you want them to choose what to east and where to sit when they arrive."

Clayton is an agency management veteran who has worked with numerous multinational brands prior to this role at Ritz-Carlton, so it is significant when he recognizes that the biggest difference in marketing today is access. In other words, marketers now have unprecedented re-al-time access to consumers through a host of channels. He elaborates: "We can say whatever we want, whenever we want, to whomever we want—which is very powerful. But there is a downside. When we abuse this power, we face more government regulation and consumer tune-out. The power is in our hands to manage this privilege properly as we move forward, so that we can keep these lines of communication open."

Clayton Ruebensaal also realizes that today even the most sophis-ticated marketer still has to be a *student of marketing*, a contemporary reality that can be overwhelming to even industry veterans. "Everything changes so quickly that you can't hold onto old rules of marketing and assume they will work today or tomorrow. You need to expose yourself to the cutting edge of what's being put into the market to find new ways to get results."

In fact, his definition of *innovation* is "doing something different enough that it carries risk of failure and the potential for unprecedent-ed success."

However, he makes a distinction between keeping current and what he considers "trend chasing." Clayton admits that managing such a shifting balance can be one of biggest frustrations with the industry at present. "The insecure among us feel the need to do every new thing without evaluating how right it is for their brand and their strategy. Some new things may be right, others not right. Meanwhile there are just as many innovative things being done with traditional mediums as with new ones. Television has never been more targeted. As email has grown out of control, direct mail is now a far less cluttered space to break through. I recently saw an incredible campaign from Kit-Kat that used print and an old fashioned 800 number that consumers interacted with by pressing the number pad. It was refreshingly simple and broke through the clutter without using the ubiquitous hashtag."

In fact, he says that he'd characterize "the reinvention of marketing" as simply "cutting through the clutter." He adds, "As new levels of fragmentation and innovation continually become accepted industry norms, the harder it is to get your message noticed. Brands need to focus on cutting through the clutter today-- more than ever."

He adds that his own small contribution to reshaping marketing is "to put more eggs into fewer baskets—in an effort to engage consumers at a *deeper* level with like-minded publishers."

Clayton outlines his own strategies for executing this focused ideal: "At the Ritz-Carlton we take great pride in scouring our markets and understanding our marketing opportunities first hand. WeChat in China, SnapChat in the USA, navigating a Blackberry and iPhone at the same time in Dubai. But with all the *new new new* in the world, too often new opportunities feel like obligations. If we jumped on every new opportunity, in social media alone, we'd drown in them. Instead we are selective about what we don't participate in, and this keeps our efforts focused and allows us to achieve excellence in a smaller list of channels. For each of our key markets, we focus our budget on either one channel or one publisher and then build a lot of engaging content for that audience. In our opinion, too many advertisers try to cover all their bases, and wind up doing so in a very surface way—resulting in just one or two print ads in a publication, which are too easy to flip by."

Under Clayton Ruebensaal's leadership, The Ritz-Carlton Hotel Company's new brand platform has come to life. In fact, Ritz-Carlton prefers to think of itself as being in the business of creating memories, a high ground in the hotel business, and as a result, eschews the usual copy and imagery of immaculate rooms, pools and spas. The brand platform, "Let Us Stay With You," turns a traditional approach on its head. Rather than telling customers, "Come stay with us," The Ritz-Carlton promises an experience that will stay with their guests long after the actual stay ends. Images in print advertising are of serendipitous moments remembering a vacation or a successful business trip amid day-to-day life. Such an imprint is an invitation to return to The Ritz-Carlton simply by closing one's eyes.

Back, though, to his belief in *breaking through the clutter.* How does his upscale hotel brand differentiate itself from a marketing standpoint?

He says, "It's difficult, because our competitors are fantastic, too. For The Ritz-Carlton, it comes down to owning something true and motivating, and then communicating it in engaging ways through everything we say and do. For our brand, it's our power to create memories. We do that every day, in every hotel, in every department, all over the world. Owning memories has been very good to us, because it's the high ground of what luxury travelers are paying for. (All luxury hotels are great-looking with attentive service.) And memories is a very interesting and imaginative subject, so it's led to very good creative."

Establishing a consistent global image for a hotel company is never easy, particularly as some properties in parts of the world may vary from certain expectations. Flexibility by country is always possible, but the key question is again whether local variations help to build that consistent global image.

Nonetheless, Clayton emphasizes that "The strategic idea must stay the same. Yes, the execution varies greatly from country to country. Our marketing about the power of memories in Japan last year centered on three photographers bringing a simple brief to life: capture memories at The Ritz-Carlton however you see fit. We then used that content online, in print, and at our hotels. It was stunning and interesting in how different they all were, but that they still all laddered back to memories and to The Ritz-Carlton."

The portraits were recreations of powerful memories that guests had recalled during a previous visit to one of the company's Japanese properties, and how those memories had stayed with them ever since. The Ritz-Carlton partnered with a leading lifestyle magazine to create portraits of guests at each of the hotels, rather than simply run print ads.

One of Clayton's greatest leadership traits is his tireless passion for the brand in support of bringing the idea of powerful memories to life. He is constantly in contact with discipline leaders from such areas as brand experience, ecommerce, public relations, publications, retail, operations and loyalty teams, as well as his various ad agencies, He works to ensure each touch point supports the brand promise, and does so in a unique way that also builds a complete brand story.

An internationalist at heart, his approach is to design programs for each region to showcase the Ritz-Carlton "creating memories" brand platform, while also speaking to core cultural or business insights. The result is that the brand promise stays the same; however, it is brought to life uniquely for each channel and region.

For example, in the Middle East, where authentic hospitality is time-honored, the focus is on the experiences The Ritz-Carlton creates, and how the hotel honors immaculate service. This message was delivered through an augmented reality experience out of a print ad, because the GCC consumer is so mobile-focused, and was a first for that region.

In China, where affluent consumers are maturing in their knowledge and appreciation of luxury goods at an unprecedented rate, the focus is on providing the crucial back story of The Ritz-Carlton brand, its unique heritage and pedigree, and why it should be considered at the very top of the category.

In the UK, the campaign's goal is to present the brand in a modern light given lingering perceptions. Through rich media, advertorial and an event, the brand was portrayed as contemporary with a focus on user-generated content and unexpected experiences around the globe. A website shows a collection of the most memorable travel experiences from around the world, from "wow" stories to exceptional service, to a one-of-a-kind cocktail recipe.

Clayton also admits that one part of his job is getting easier as the business traveler and luxury vacationer is often the same person. "For us, someone who comes on business will come back for vacation and the overlap of the two increases every year. Most affluent consumers are comfortable with their work life and personal life blending."

He adds that today's real-time, constantly-changing Digital Age has refocused his marketing ideals for Ritz-Carlton. "The past three years have been a giant shift for us. We went from spending 20% of our advertising budget on digital, to 60%, to now we spend 60% on digital advertising and another 15% on digital content on top of that."

With over 100 years of history, beginning with the legacy of the celebrated hotelier Cesar Ritz, the "king of hoteliers and hotelier to kings," who managed The Ritz Paris and The Carlton in London, The Ritz-Carlton Hotel Company now has 86 hotels worldwide. Its properties are found in 29 countries and territories, including Aruba, Austria, Bahrain, Canada, Cayman Islands, Chile, China, Germany, India, Indonesia, Israel, Japan, Kazakhstan, Malaysia, Mexico, Oman, Portugal, Puerto Rico, Qatar, Russia, Singapore, Saudi Arabia, South Korea, Spain, Thailand, Turkey, the United Arab Emirates, U.S. Virgin Islands, and the United States.

In 1998, The Ritz-Carlton's success attracted the attention of the hospitality industry, and the company was acquired by Marriott International. Since the purchase, The Ritz-Carlton has continued to grow, and in 2000, The Ritz-Carlton Residences opened their first property in Washington, D.C., followed by their first Destination Club property,

Aspen Highlands, Colorado in 2001. In addition to dozens of new hotels around the globe, the company opened the first Ritz-Carlton Reserve property in 2008, offering a private sanctuary experience in Phulay Bay, Krabi, Thailand.

The Ritz-Carlton has always believed that being a legend requires a great story. However, if you ask Clayton Ruebensaal how one measures the success of a marketing effort, he will tell you: "Marketing success can only be measured by how well it delivered against the goals of the business." And he has done that brilliantly.

Clayton Ruebensaal leads global marketing for The Ritz-Carlton Hotel Company. He was responsible for launching their current brand platform "Let Us Stay With You" in 2011. He was named an **Internationalist of the Year** *in 2013. Since then his team has launched a new global website, a mobile app with on and off property functionality, unique websites for China and Japan, a new partnership with Mercedes-Benz China, and integrated efforts across the globe to tell the brand's amazing story to luxury consumers.*

Prior to The Ritz-Carlton, Clayton was CEO of British advertising agency Beattie McGuinness Bungay's New York office—just as BMB became agency of the year in the UK after three years in business. He also served as CEO of Cliff Freeman & Partners (2008-2009). He spent much of his career at international advertising agency BBDO as EVP, Account Director leading The Economist, Sony, Pepsi's Aquafina, and ETRADE. Early career roles included positions at Deutsch and Grey.

Clayton lives in Washington D.C. with his sons Penn and Hucksley and wife Rebecca who still needs convincing that a trip to Krabi, Thailand is considered work.

Dana Anderson

of Mondelēz Embraces Marketing Reinvention through Creativity and Collaboration

Dana Anderson
Senior Vice President & Chief Marketing Officer
Mondelēz International
Deerfield, Illinois USA

FAST FACTS
Where were you born?
Owenton, Kentucky. Because, the much smaller town in which we lived did not have a hospital. This explains so much.

Was there a lesson you learned in an early first job that still applies now?
My first job was selling bras and girdles of which I had little need or experience. My lesson was how to sell something even if you were not the target audience. Strongest memory: A woman marching up to the counter, opening up her blouse so that I could study her bra. "Do you have anything like this?" she barked. "No, ma'am, I certainly do not," was my humble reply.

What was your big career break?
My first big speech. No one ever looked at me the same way after that. The experience transformed my career and changed the way I thought about the power of storytelling.

Are you willing to admit your biggest career mistake? (Or at least the one you learned the most from!)
No. That's what I learned from my biggest career mistake.

What's your favorite city for business travel?
It is a toss-up between London and Buenos Aires. I feel dreamy and transported in both.

What's your favorite place in the world?
My kitchen.

THERE'S NO QUESTION THAT THROUGHOUT HER
CAREER, Dana Anderson has been an advocate for
extraordinary quality and relevance in advertising.
She's also managed to embrace the new with appar-
ent ease, while constantly challenging convention—
and sometimes *big* convention. Never shy about
questioning the status quo, she has become the de
facto champion for work that resonates with today's
consumers. If anyone is at the center of the continual
evolution of marketing, or its *reinvention*—given today's breathless pace—it's Dana.

At the end of September 2014, Mondelēz International announced
her appointment as Senior Vice President and Chief Marketing Officer
of the multibillion dollar snacking powerhouse with brands like *Oreo*,
LU and *Nabisco* biscuits; *Cadbury, Cadbury Dairy Milk* and *Milka* chocolate; *Trident* gum; *Halls* candy and *Tang* powdered beverages, and an
extraordinary foothold in 165 countries. Frankly, there is no better can-
didate for a 21st century CMO. She once noted that executive recruiter
Korn Ferry said that the most vital characteristic of the modern CMO is
learning agility. Dana Anderson possesses that rare ability to not only
embrace change, but to realize that past success has little to do with
navigating in the present, and certainly not in the future.

So how does she make sense of the business of marketing—right
now?

Her recent presentations provide a mosaic of ideas as she chooses
to regularly tackle issues that cause the industry to stop and think—on
several levels. Her editorial in *The Wall Street Journal* in March fueled
a debate about the role of Agencies of Record, called *AORs are No*

Longer the Pathway to Oz for Clients or Agencies. (And the article advocated "Saying Goodbye to the Yellow Brick Road.") A June Cannes Ad Festival discussion on Blue Whales and Hummingbirds may have captured people's imaginations through a fanciful title, but its message of how big marketers and independent agencies can work together continued to question existing client and agency infrastructures as the industry moves forward. New York Advertising Week's panel entitled "Fearless" not only featured Dana, but pitted "classical marketing" against "chaos" to reflect the realities of functioning in an always-on, socially transparent and accountable digital age.

Dana Anderson knows that when we strive to embrace the future, "things get messy." She characterizes today's marketing dynamic as the reduction of time and the expansion of channels through digital means. (She has said often that "digital just didn't make one new channel—it created thousands of new mediums.") Ideally, this requires not only a new way of working, but also a diverse group of creative contributors who can thrive amid change and chaos. And she reminds us, "Creativity in all of its forms is vital to consumers, so it's vital to us."

She says, "More people are playing a part in the marketing of a brand. Today, we need a rich chorus of people to solve problems, jump higher, work faster, and collaborate better. This is a new community of creators, strategists, entertainers, content providers, production houses, and social media companies, plus many others with varied skills sets, who collectively have a seat at the table and can face a challenge together by adding capabilities that can meet shifting demands."

And while the community that serves the brand is larger than ever before and requires many new kinds of creative partnerships, managing the brand is harder. This is particularly true if a brand is part of big corporation that loves proof and prides itself on control and measurement. Dana suggests that "We now have to work with 'strategic intuition,' or 'studied improvisation'-- a combination of right and left brain functions. Whatever we do, we have to find a way to include this diversity of contributors to be part of the brand story." She adds that younger people are often more comfortable with this form of working—perhaps the result of "growing up social" or simply accepting a "hacking" culture of shared problem solving.

In fact, Dana believes that the acceptance of iteration offers great opportunity, but it can also generate considerable challenges for people who are used to being in charge. "Of course, we have to embrace iteration—today's world requires that we continually 'throw out and learn.' The tough part is that no one is going to fully understand every step the process. We just can't know it all. Perhaps we can learn it, but then we're up against that time and breadth continuum of today's tech world. We have to bring together many varied collaborators today to fully solve a problem."

Dana cites a fascinating Mondelēz Fly Garage creative session in Argentina to underscore the shift that's necessary when executing cooperative solutions. She outlines how people of different disciplines were brought together to work on a creative idea. "However, we introduced made a rule that you could only love your idea for 3 hours. Given how my generation of creatives grew up, this was heresy, as so much of their identity and creative stamp was 'This was MY idea!' We must recognize that the more consumers engage with brands, the greater the opportunity for new types of collaborative creative ideas." As she mentioned in her Advertising Week "Fearless" program when referring to a new culture of social media sharing and advocacy, "If it's not good enough to tell somebody about, then it's not good enough for your brand."

According to Dana Anderson, "The business of the business needs to be renovated."

She says, "I honestly don't understand why we as an industry would think that models from 50 years ago should continue to work well given today's pace, complexity and just how much has changed in half a century! That's not to say that there aren't classic elements that can work in real time. We must carry forward the best what's classic, particularly important issues regarding brand purpose, promise, and the commitment to never betray the covenant a brand makes with a consumer. However, these issues are about ethos, not about structure, functions and new models for the business."

Without question, Dana believes there are opportunities for a new way forward. "Marketers are 50% of this dance, and we have to learn to be better clients by innovating and finding improved ways of working. There's no doubt that agencies today have challenges—from creating new staffing with different skills, to coping with clients who continually revise plans, to the sheer number of things on the table to insure they meet needs, to financial obligations with holding companies. If we change the way we come together, the outcome can only be better."

Marketers, she feels, are optimists. "We work toward solutions and keep evolving. Marketing is part of culture, and culture is always changing—and will never be the same again. There's an important message for those who are lamenting the old way of working: this should be a time of celebration and excitement about a new ways of working."

Of course, moving toward any new structure is uncomfortable for most people. Finding alternative approaches to working with different partners isn't easy either. However, Dana urges that the industry fix what's not working, as she states in her *Wall Street Journal* editorial, "As clients, we have a responsibility and an opportunity to lead the way to a better place."

She accepts that a transition will start when more clients introduce new programs and model different behavior. "Change will occur faster than we anticipate as marketers will ultimately request new ways of working to leverage a community against a single purpose, over a prescribed period of time, with decision-making on the client side, and supported by data."

She adds, "If you want inspiration from the power of change, go to San Francisco. We just attended a meeting there about wearable technology, and I was charmed by a purse that also charges a phone or an iPad! How wonderfully practical and terrific! Go talk to the folks in Silicon Valley, and you'll look at the world in different way. After spending some time there, you can't possibly think the world is dark."

Mondelēz is also working differently to drive innovation and leadership in its approach to creativity and collaboration. One initiative, Project Sprout, has encouraged smaller agencies to quickly develop digital campaigns for the company's gum business, which includes *Trident*, the world's biggest gum brand, for the US and other regions of the world. A partnership with video-news provider NowThisNews is helping the company respond faster to pop-culture and news to create relevant content for *Oreos*, *Wheat Thins* and *Halls*. This involves the resources of Blink Studios, the real-time production company developed with NowThisNews. Plus, *Oreos*' "Snack Hacks" program is well underway and features a video series with top chefs who "remix" new varieties of cookies.

Some of these themes of innovation were echoed in her Advertising Week "Fearless" panel, which underscored how risk-taking is critical today if a brand is to resonate with contemporary customers. Sometimes those risks result in failure or even letting go a portion of a brand's audience. To quote Dana Anderson, "being fearless is the only answer right now. If you play it right up the middle, you really don't achieve much."

Interestingly, Dana Anderson knows something about overcoming fear, and the story of her own beginning in the industry is now as legendary as it is inspirational.

In the early 80's while working at a Chicago ad agency, she joined her boss in a new business meeting. Just prior to her portion of the presentation, she got nervous and fainted. Of course, the irony of the story is that today Dana is one of the industry's most sought-after speakers, because the combination of her ideas, refreshing approach to emotionally-charged truths, down-to-earth style, and memorable axioms have made a significant impact on redirecting, and yes, renovating, "the business of the business." She often says that what she learned from that early incident was to shift from she felt, and focus instead on what the client, or the client's brand, needed.

Some lessons stay with you forever.

Dana Anderson is the Senior Vice President and Chief Marketing Officer of Mondelēz International and is responsible for the company's global portfolio of advertising, media and marketing partners and oversees the teams who manage Agency Relations, Brand Equity, Brand Strategy, Marketing Capabilities, Media and Digital for the company's global and regional brands.

A 25-year advertising veteran, she was named to her previous position of SVP Marketing Communication and Strategy when Mondelez International was created in 2012, having held the same role when she joined Kraft Foods in 2009. Prior to that, she served as President and CEO at DDB Chicago. She started her career at Young & Rubicam and then moved to J. Walter Thompson. Dana was also President and CEO of Foote, Cone & Belding, Chicago, until leaving there to join DDB in 2004.

On Nov. 13, 2014, the Advertising Club of New York plans to honor Anderson as its "Advertising Person of the Year." In 2012, she was identified as one of the "100 Most Influential Women in Advertising" by Ad Age, and she was also the winner of the Ad Women of New York's "Changing the Game" award.

In 2001, Dana was named "Advertising Woman of the Year" by the Chicago Advertising Federation for her many contributions to the industry. She is on the board of the Association of National Advertisers and is a member of The Chicago Network.

PURPOSE:
Instilling Purpose through New Actions

Fernando Chacon

Revolutionizing Itaú's Marketing to "Change People's World for the Better"

Fernando Chacon
Chief Marketing Officer
Itaú Unibanco
São Paulo, Brazil

FAST FACTS
Where were you born?
São Paulo, SP—Brazil

Was there a lesson you learned in an early first job that still applies now?
Be disciplined.

What is the best advice you were ever given?
Do everything with passion and dedication. Even the simplest tasks.

Are you willing to admit your biggest career mistake? (Or at least the one you learned the most from!)
There's no doubt I made mistakes and learned so much, but I always prefer to learn from the mistakes of others.

What's your favorite city for business travel?
New York

What's your favorite place in the world?
My house or wherever my family is.

FERNANDO CHACON IS A NEW KIND OF GLOBAL MARKETER. A native of Brazil, his values embrace a new world ethos. He believes that successful brands increasingly will be those built for people, particularly in a social media world. Fernando is fond of saying, "We must be guided by our brand proposition and business vision, while keeping the dialogue flowing with people."

He believes that marketing professionals must continuously increase their knowledge about their consumers. "This is what makes a difference today, and it will be increasingly so in the future. The world is changing at a fast pace, and so are people. To understand the meaning of these changes, their impact on people's lives, and, as result, how they can change the way we think, feel and react, is the critical challenge for new marketing professionals, wherever they operate."

Significantly, he adds, "Today, people expect more from brands. They expect something that goes beyond the customary rational relationship. People want to have something to believe in. They want to be inspired and connected by a purpose, and then embrace that leading, aspirational role model. When we as marketers have a clear understanding of this situation, everything changes. We leave behind self-focused strategies and one-way speeches, and instead, evolve towards true conversation. Strong, relevant, inspiring content will become the topic of many conversations, whether over the web or over bar tables. People are becoming more social and engaged; today's marketers will only become successful when they understand the importance of this trend."

Certainly, Fernando Chacon is at the forefront of understanding this trend as demonstrated by the extraordinary success of Itaú Unibanco's

"Great Transformation" advertising for the recent FIFA World Cup™ in Brazil. Not only does the spectacular film transform the country into a giant soccer stadium that unifies a nation and embraces the world, but Brazil's president praised the spot—perhaps an act only possible in a country where passion about great advertising is the norm. The bank certainly demonstrated its belief in the power of Brazilians to "change the game"—not simply as World Cup hosts, but as participants in building their own modern country. And this epic, stirring campaign had tremendous benefits for Itaú.

Fernando explains, "The film 'The Great Transformation' was a milestone for us and one of our best advertising moments—an unforgettable one, I would say. The film was part of a greater project developed by Itaú for the FIFA World Cup™ in Brazil. The question was: how would a bank placed in the third layer of FIFA's sponsors compete on equal terms with global consumer brands that had the advantage of being master sponsors of the competition? To face this challenge, we carried out a long-term plan and sought to achieve a perfect performance by using a great deal of real-time information particularly from social networks—enabling a new approach to creation in a continuous and cooperative process."

He adds humbly, "I will admit that we exceeded our own expectations. Our song became the anthem of Brazilian rooters, with over 300 thousand downloads. We also received more than 1,500 videos spontaneously uploaded by average citizens. Our communications surpassed 58 million views and 42 million interactions in social media. We reached the greatest peak of engagement in Twitter's history in Brazil. We were the brand most associated with the Brazilian national team, and the second most associated with the World Cup, second only to Coca-Cola."

Fernando Chacon also believes this inspiring effort also helped "to strengthen our brand and connect it more closely to our consumers and all people swept up in the passion of the moment and the message." Interestingly, he notes that the effort provided a tremendous lesson for the marketing team and the advertising agency by understanding that there is a new model to be followed—one he describes as "more lively, focused and connected with the feeling and the mood of people." He also recognizes that a big part of Itaú's mission is to present a new Global Latin America to the world, while deepening its roots at home.

Certainly, Brazil is on the mind of every global marketing executive today. The country enjoys an international reputation for producing some of the world's most creative advertising, and largely continues with a full-service agency structure. Ad Executives also achieve celebrity status in Brazil, while the Brazilian public enjoys and admires advertising, especially when it is entertaining. The power of technology and connectedness cannot be underestimated; just last year, *The Wall Street Journal* called Brazil: "The Social Media Capital of the Universe."

So does having origins in Brazil—one of the most creative, pro-advertising and socially-connected nations on earth—make a difference in Fernando Chacon's approach to marketing?

His answer is straightforward: "It is always important to understand the context within which we operate and, especially, where we find opportunities for differentiation. Brazil has unique cultural characteristics that were developed throughout our history. I think that being creative was not a choice, nor is it necessarily a characteristic of a generation. Rather, our creativity is a form of survival for people in a very young, developing country in search of a place in the sun in a strongly competitive world. If we consider the universe of marketing, we see that being born in such a culture with its strong social connections may, indeed, bring advantages—although this is not sufficient."

He asserts: "What makes a difference today is the way the brand thinks and the things it believes in. Yes, this has a lot to do with its country of origin or the country in which it operates, but the brand's DNA and the purpose of its actions matter most. Itaú, for example, believes in high-quality, strongly creative advertising, which it has been consistently pursuing for over 40 years. This, of course, brings us some legacies and the possibility to build extremely proprietary brand codes, as well as a connection to people that goes beyond our relationship to basic, core activities."

Fernando's progressive views are uncommon for a bank marketer. He talks about a brand proposition that is both "heartwarming and relevant in the lives of people." Such language is rarely associated with financial institutions or even the broader corporate world.

However, Fernando Chacon is adamant in his vision for the bank: "The purpose of Itaú is to 'change people's world for the better.' My greatest challenge is to make this purpose more present in the organization-- in everything it does, and especially, in the way it communicates with people. Of course, this is affected by today's business ideals and a new generation of shared value for all stakeholders-- our employees, our customers, our shareholders and society. It is widely known that companies and people that focus on a purpose achieve greater success in the long term, whether regarding market value or the differentiated relationship they establish with people.

What we have seen at Itaú is that people who experience the brand's sweet and more inspiring side—a result of our convictions and investments in important human causes—have a more intense and promising relationship with the bank. By encouraging our customers to replace their cars with bicycles, to read for a child, or to improve their knowledge of arts and culture, we are fostering the individual's capacity through education. We are betting on the idea that, with stronger critical awareness, these individuals will not only become better citizens, but also customers who will be more prepared to make their best decisions-- with independence and conviction in their financial lives, today and tomorrow."

Fernando Chacon also sees the notion of transformation as key to both his bank and to Brazil as Latin America becomes a more essential part of the global economy—for its dynamic growth markets, as well as its innovative companies. In addition to the now famous World Cup spot, "transforming the world" is the inspiration for Itaú's marketing principles, as well as its corporate ethos. In an effort to encourage Brazilian society to transform itself, the bank supports efforts around education, culture, sports, and urban mobility.

As if these humanistic ideals aren't ambitious enough, Itaú strives to meet additional goals by being the leading bank in sustainable performance and customer satisfaction. Fernando comments, "I would say that our vision fully relates to our belief in win-win relationships and the understanding that our growth is based on the growth and generation of value to our employees, shareholders, customers, society and the country – this is what we call 'shared value.'"

São Paulo-based Itaú Unibanco Holding S.A, is the result of a 2008 merger of Banco Itaú and Unibanco. Today, Itaú is the largest bank in Latin America and among the world's largest banks by market value with operations in 20 countries throughout the Americas, Asia and Europe.

For almost a decade, Itaú has been the most valuable brand name in Brazil, according to Interbrand. When asked how he consistently achieves this, Fernando answers with characteristic candor, while painting an undeniably clear description of his motivation: "The strength of a brand relies on the balance between tangible and intangible assets, or between the success we have today and our capacity to achieve success tomorrow. This is what we believe, and it is also how we manage our greatest asset: our brand. By properly defining and aligning this brand vision within the organization, everyone becomes a partner in insuring the success of this mission. A brand is comprised of details—both everything we do or don't do. And the way we do or don't do things can add a brick, or even remove several bricks, from our daily construction."

Fernando Chacon combines his idealism for the bank's values with a realism about marketing's current challenges. He admits that one of his biggest struggles as a marketer is finding ways to be relevant when his customers are constantly connected as they face an overabundance of information and a scarcity of time.

His solution? "We have to be more creative, and, at the same time, more truthful and transparent. Technology is a very important advantage, but, in this context, it must go hand-in-hand with simplicity. It must be an enabling tool, that is, a means, instead of a solution itself. Doing marketing today is quite different from what it was a few years ago. Now marketing is much more in the hands of consumers than marketing professionals, and it is this precise understanding that may or may not make a difference for a brand."

Innovation is a term more regularly applied to marketing; however, Fernando's views on the subject are provocative. He says, "Innovation is often confused with a solution in search for a problem. In my opinion, today innovation can be defined in two ways. The first is as simple as doing basic things well. People are always asking for that—our consumers ask us not to complicate, to be simple and deliver what we have promised. This is, by itself, an innovation for a brand today. The second is to use technology to get closer, instead of growing more distant—again to simplify instead of making things more complicated.

People don't need to be knowledgeable about technology; it is technology that needs to enhance its knowledge about people."

So what's Fernando Chacon's vision for the future? "I believe that the future of marketing is absolutely linked to the future of people. Our challenge is being connected, understanding context, and changing as fast as our consumers and their world. And doing this—while grounded in a strong brand purpose—will make all the difference."

Fernando Chacon joined Itaú Unibanco in 2008, and was named an **Internationalist of the Year** *in 2013 for his extraordinary marketing contributions of worldwide significance. He was also the first Brazilian marketer to be named to this list since it origins in 2004.*

Prior to Itaú, he was involved in related banking and credit card marketing roles. He spent seven years as the Vice President of Marketing for Credicard, originally founded by Itaú, Citigroup and Unibanco, in the 1970s. (Interestingly, in 2013, Itaú reclaimed Credicard from Citigroup through a USD $1.3 billion acquisition which provided the bank with an additional 10% share of Brazil's credit card market.) His earlier positions includes roles with Redecard, the payment processor, also now owned by Itaú, and Cândia Supermercados.

Zita Cassizzi

Discusses TOMS' Sustainable Giving Through Business in a Digital World...

Zita Cassizzi
Chief Digital Officer
TOMS Shoes
Santa Monica, California USA

FAST FACTS
Where were you born?
I was born and grew up in Budapest, Hungary.

Was there a lesson you learned in an early first job that still applies now?
My first job was working in the graduate school at the University of Texas' Center for Management Systems. In 1990, it really was the start of the internet era, and this was a fantastic opportunity for me to explore the booming changes of technology from the academic side while I was studying business. Lessons learned? Take every opportunity with the job and in the connection to the job to learn as much as possible!

What is the best advice you were ever given?
Instead of getting stuck in problems, always focus on creating solutions and new opportunities.

What was your big career break?
In 1995, I joined Dell and was hired by a fantastic leader in a hyper-growth environment, full of opportunities.

Where do you turn for inspiration?
Art, Science and kids. Absorbing and learning all new things and new ways of thinking.

What's your favorite city for business travel?
London.

What's your favorite place in the world?
The hills and lakes of the Alps in Bavaria, Austria and Italy.

ASK ZITA CASSIZZI IF TOMS IS CHANGING THE WORLD, and she'll tell you that business has the power to make an incredible difference—both at scale and in the day-to-day lives of many of the world's poorest citizens. In fact, she'd argue that business is the only way to create the means to give sustainably. TOMS, the rapidly-expanding One-for-One giving company, has awakened many companies to think beyond the basics of corporate social responsibility.

Zita's role as Chief Digital Officer is essential to growing the TOMS business globally, particularly in a world where both loyal supporters and potential new customers embrace social media, mobile, and digital content. She believes that the prevalence of digital communication channels is not only shaping the speed and connectedness of our world, but is also dramatically influencing consumer behavior and expectations.

"My DNA," she says, "is all about the direct business model with a hyper-focus on delivering a unique customer experience. I'm motivated by the fast pace of technology and how it empowers the world. It's exciting being close to this change and creating some portion of it. The fusion of digital and physical experiences is not only shaping our business practices, but affecting social and economic environments. This phenomenon is fascinating, and I love being a part of this change."

Founded in 2006 by Texas entrepreneur Blake Mycoskie, TOMS represents the evolution of a new business model of increasing interest in today's socially-responsible world. TOMS is a for-profit company that sells shoes, eyewear and coffee with a giving component. When the company sells a pair of shoes, for example, a second pair is given to a child in need. One for One. The giving shoes are shipped to a recipient country, where an NGO partner picks them up, transports them to their community, and distributes the shoes to children in need. And California-based TOMS currently gives in 70 countries.

To date, over 35 million pairs of shoes have been given to children in need through humanitarian organizations that incorporate shoes into their community development programs. The shoes may be used as a trigger to encourage parents to take children to clinics, or enable kids to attend school, or prevent illness in a country like Ethiopia where medical groups are working to raise awareness of podoconiosis, a disfiguring foot disease prevented by simply wearing shoes. In concert with Save the Children, TOMS has given 100,000 pairs of shoes to displaced Syrians at the Zaatari refugee camp in Jordan.

TOMS is now creating local jobs by manufacturing shoes in a number of countries where they give—Kenya, India, and Haiti, where an artist collective is customizes TOMS shoes for a specialty line. In fact, TOMS has made a commitment to produce one-third of its Giving shoes locally by the end of 2015, and they're on track to accomplish this goal. The company is also producing other types of shoes of use in different terrains, climates and seasons, such as winter boots for markets like Afghanistan, Kyrgyzstan, Nepal, Tajikistan, as well as India and Pakistan.

The original TOMS shoes are based on Argentina's *alpargata* design, and part of the TOMS' logo incorporates the Argentinian flag, emphasizing the roots of the company's giving efforts. The name TOMS itself refers to shoes for a better tomorrow or *TOM*orrow *S*hoes.

Since 2011, TOMS has also been selling eyewear, and again helping to improve or restore the eyesight of people in the developing world— directly helping over 250,000 individuals in 10 countries through various vision programs. TOMS has trademarked the term One for One®, and will likely expand the concept to products outside the lifestyle-fashion space, as they have done recently with coffee, or "Coffee for You; Water for All." With each purchase of a bag of TOMS coffee, the company provides one week of clean water to a person in need. To date, TOMS has helped give over 37,000 weeks of safe water n 5 countries through Water for People.

Few brands have managed to combine for-profit business with a level of accessible philanthropy that underscores a genuine spirit of giving. TOMS has achieved success and admiration, because its model has the potential to do enormous good. Yet the company is also built with a passionate entrepreneurial business sense and strong 21st century marketing principles. (And it didn't hurt that the worlds of fashion and entertainment immediately embraced the brand; even style icon and designer Karl Lagerfeld admitted his early adoption of TOMS!)

As TOMS' Chief Digital Officer, Zita has a pivotal role with global responsibility for direct and digital businesses and consumer experience. This includes a daunting list of concerns: E-commerce business management, online marketing, mobile and social media, web development and analytics, testing and targeting, digital business development, as well as retail outlets, customer service and support. She characterizes the role as placing her "in a fortunate position to oversee our direct consumer life cycle and touch points from A to Z."

While Zita leads all things digital, she admits, "My focus is on creating and growing our digital and direct business globally. It is critical for TOMS to establish compelling, unique, and accessible experiences for our consumers±no matter where they are physically. This means observing, listening and leading with a focus on consumer behavior in all points of engagement and in all points of commerce—from awareness to consideration to loyalty to physical and experiential integration."

Zita emphasizes that everything TOMS does is digital. She has outlined what she calls "The 5Cs," a guide to embrace the digital future and create an effective omni-channel marketing strategy. "These are not approaches," she emphasizes, "but what we think about every single day at TOMS."

Connect with your community

Zita talks of TOMS as a *movement-based* business, which means that understanding the values of both current and future customers is especially important in establishing true community. She believes that "today's customers expect you to be where they are—at any moment." A majority of TOMS' customers are Millennials who have been rapidly spreading the word, particularly as 83% have a smartphone that they use to post, share, update, and upload daily.

She admits that the biggest recent marketing change she's experienced is TOMS' shift "to start reaching our consumers via Mobile first. Nearly all of our consumers carry a smartphone and are connected 24/7. We coined the phrase 'mocial' around the office to ensure that everyone from developers to operations folks are thinking about our mobile and social strategy-- which is how our consumers live."

Zita also talks about "the modern landscape of engagement at the intersection of technology and human emotion." TOMS is a human-based business in that it works to improve people's lives through business, and, in doing so, also delivers human emotion. According to Zita, the two go hand I hand. "There are no greater engagement touch points that the TOMS Giving Trips where employees and partners go into the field to work with NGOs who distribute the TOMS products." Zita herself has been to orphanages and schools in the Ukraine and the Crimea on recent trips and can't say enough about the community outreach and the overwhelming emotions that arise from caring for the neglected and experiencing how lives can be changed with a few simple basics.

She's now working to capture the emotion of these Giving Trips in the TOMS retail experience—both online and offline. Her Chief Digital Officer role also means that she manages TOMS' retail expansion; stores are now open in Venice, California and Austin, Texas, and are soon planned for New York City , Chicago and Portland, Oregon. "Recreating the emotion and significance of the Giving Trips is part of our ecosystem. We are working with the physical and the experiential to show how the brand touches you and makes a connection with the TOMS community."

Content

Although content is an overworked word in contemporary marketing, at TOMS it simply means delivering meaningful and multidimensional content about all products and services that a manner that is both relevant and valuable to its customers. "We ask ourselves every day: What is valuable to customers—*intrinsically and extrinsically*? This is not only about discounts and coupons, but about more essential customer needs—as many buy our products to contribute to making a difference in the world. Value is not only expressed in products and service, but in internal satisfaction."

Zita is also working to extend these elements of content and value into the TOMS retails stores. She wants shoppers to experience many elements of a Giving Trip while in store, and also view inspiring content from other members of the TOMS community. Customers can vote on these content submissions to determine candidates to accompany the team on an upcoming Giving Trip.

Customer relationships for life

When Zita thinks about the reinvention of marketing, she's convinced that "Marketing *per se* in the traditional sense is now too one dimensional to meet today's demands. We should always be thinking about long-term relationship building with our consumers. My philosophy: create trust through open dialogues with consumers via those channels that they want to use to engage with us.

We often adopt the tone of voice as best friend—honest, inspirational, humble. But it's not that simple. Customers need change. Sometimes they simply prefer to connect with something factual about a One for One product. If your goal is to keep customer relationships for life, then you have to be multidimensional."

Continuing the conversation

Listening and adapting is also a big factor in keeping customers for life. According to Zita, "We certainly listen in social media; however, the TOMS organization is designed so that customer service is integrated in all we do, particularly in terms of listening to our customers. We encourage our customer services representation to spend more time talking with customers, so we can learn the ways in which their purchase matters. Of course, this is a business and there need to be a resolution to the purpose of their call, but a longer handling time has taught us much about how we better serve the needs of our customers and keep them loyal. Campus club and community clubs have also been tremendously helpful for listening and helping us adapt to consumer interests.

Create culture of innovation

""We have a term at TOMS," says Zita, "it's **TTF—T**ry It, **T**est It and **F**ail (*fast*). This attitude fosters out of box thinking." She describes how this concept enabled the launch last November of TOMS' Marketplace, a new platform to inspire customers to start businesses. TOMS Marketplace curates and sells online the products of social entrepreneurs who are doing good with craft items ranging from jewelry to accessories to clothing to home goods and more. This digital go-to-market strategy aggregates willing buyers around the world who are delight to find such items and also support such ventures. One of the Marketplace entrepreneurs employs India's unemployable for a block printing process, another creates opportunity for 100+ women in Northern Uganda who turn recycled paper into a line of colorful jewelry.

"These individuals," says Zita, "are teaching us new ways to think and make a difference. They are helping us consider how we can evolve as a business and a company. This digital window is the future of retail. We want to embrace what is impactful and fosters community, and in so doing, improve people's lives through business."

Given the phenomenon of TOMS and Zita's complex digital role, I asked her how she defines *innovation*—unquestionably an essential component of the TOMS brand. Her answer was immediate: "Innovation is no longer just another ingredient in business success or a prescribed 10% of a job function. Innovation—whether in the evolution of ideas, the effectiveness of operations, new ways of solving an existing challenge, or experimenting with a completely new concept—is necessary in our 'Digital Age.' In today's world, we have great technologies with extreme levels of computing power, but an even higher level of human innovation, as well as imagination and inspiration, remains critical to deploying this technology in the most impactful way." And we have no doubt that Zita will continue to bring that balance to TOMS and to the evolution of contemporary business ideals.

Zita Cassizzi was named a 2013 **Internationalist of the Year** *for her global work at TOMS.*

Prior to TOMS, sheled Dell.com globally. As the vice president of Dell's Global Online organization, she was responsible for all aspects of Dell.com, including its long-term strategy, creative and user design, content creation, and social media efforts. She also oversaw the operational management of Dell.com including digital marketing, behavioral targeting and web analytics.

Before serving as global vice president of Dell.com, Zita was head of marketing and general manager of Dell's Global Consumer Online business. In this capacity, she expanded the global online operations and drove significant growth in conversion and site visits while managing a global P&L of close to $5 billion.

Zita also spent two years in Europe as a member of the European management team leading the Software & Peripheral business. In this role, she oversaw the management and marketing of software and accessories. With her leadership, Dell launched its first printer line of business, including consumables across Europe, and refined the sales, marketing and operations strategy resulting in doubling the revenue and expanding profits to double-digit operating income.

Morten Albæk

of Vestas Rewrites
the Rules of Business
Marketing for
a Transparent,
Connected World

Morten Albæk

*CMO and Group Senior Vice President
for Global Marketing, Communication
& Corporate Relations*
Vestas Wind Systems
Aarhus, Denmark

FAST FACTS

Where were you born?
*I was born in Uggerby, Denmark. Uggerby
is a very small town at the northern tip of
Denmark. In fact, Uggerby is such a small
town that most Danes have never heard
of it.*

*Was there a lesson you learned in an early
first job that still applies now?*
The most important lesson I have learned and that still applies today is that you
need to find meaningfulness in what you do. One should never be afraid to leave a
priviledged life for a meaningful one if the privileged one is meaningless. Bringing
meaningfulness to your life and meaning in what you do is the only way to live, to be
happy and to be successful.

What is the best advice you were ever given?
Believing in yourself is only half as powerful as knowing yourself .

What was your big career break?
I have never had a pause or break in my career and don't plan on having one before
I retire.

*Are you willing to admit your biggest career mistake? (Or at least the one you
learned the most from!)*
That I once accepted to work 12 months for a manager that neither professionally
nor existentialistically could teach me anything. Instead, I should have resigned after
working 12 hours for him.

Where do you turn for inspiration?
I am easily inspired. There is not a moment in my life where I am not observing what
is around me. I travel a lot and I find inspiration wherever I go as being confronted
to new ideas, new people and new realities always inspire me.

What's your favorite city for business travel?
The location where I travel to doesn't matter, but the people I meet and whom inspire me are key. You can find incredible people and new sources of inspiration in all parts of the world, whether it is in New York City or in a small community in Kenya. All you need to do is to be open minded and be ready to be surprised and inspired.

What's your favorite place in the world?
Home with my two kids Emilia and Asger will always be my favorite place in this world. There is nothing more satisfying and meaningful than coming home to your loved ones.

MORTEN ALBÆK IS THE CHARISMATIC CHAMPION OF THE WORLD'S LARGEST RENEWABLE ENERGY COMPANY, Vestas Wind Systems. A well-known business personality in his native Denmark and increasingly the world, he manages to be both an idealist and pragmatist who is unabashedly outspoken, often controversial, but always devoted to new ways of thinking about the value and purpose of marketing. He is responsible for leading the transformation of wind turbine manufacturing company Vestas Wind Systems A/S from a product-oriented company to a global B-to-B-to-C brand.

Albæk also views himself as a Corporate Philosopher—a rare designation for a global CMO who is not yet 40 years old. He believes that if wind power is to play a significant role in the world's future energy mix, it will not gain acceptance through traditional business and political channels, but through the power and extraordinary resources of contemporary marketing.

Since joining Vestas in 2009, one can easily see the dramatic progression and sophistication of his marketing thinking, along with his growing confidence in greater risk-taking with larger projects. Morten Albæk's recent initiative, *Wind of Prosperity,* is not only a sweeping gesture; it has the capability of rewriting the very essence of purposeful marketing.

Announced in December 2013, *Wind for Prosperity* is a global initiative based on an innovative commercial business model to provide electricity to the world's remote communities and ensure long-term, sustainable economic development. The project's initial goal is to deploy wind energy that provides electricity for 100 communities or roughly one million people within the next three years.

Vestas' larger mission, though, is to end energy poverty with the potential to deliver affordable electricity to app. 100 million people in remote, high-wind areas worldwide, while providing a risk-adjusted return to investors. The initiative is now underway through the collaboration of the United Nations and Dr. Sultan Ahmed Al Jaber, Managing Director and CEO of Masdar, Abu Dhabi's renewable energy company and Sir Richard Branson's Carbon War Room organization.

Sir Richard Branson has called the concept "an interesting example of how innovative commercial ideas can be born out of social or environmental challenges."

The origins of *Wind for Prosperity* literally came from an insight Morten had last year. He knew that approximately 1.3 billion people today live without reliable access to electricity. He also realized that Vestas has the ability to identify areas of the world where wind resources can be exploited at low cost in remote-access locations. Albæk and his team discovered that around 100 million people are living in areas of high poverty with abundant wind resources. Wind for Prosperity was born when Vestas recognized that rural, off-grid communities could experience sustainable prosperity by harvesting the wind in an economically-viable manner.

Morten Albæk's *Wind for Prosperity* concept demonstrates how companies can embrace big, sustainable ideas with innovative marketing strategies that connect deeply with customers' passions and values. These programs go beyond charitable giving, Corporate Social Responsibility projects, "green" initiatives, or even cause-related ventures. They are simply CENTRAL to marketing ideals and new business models. When done right, these initiatives result in growth and in literally making a difference in the world.

Today's social media environment with its constant sharing, commentary, advocacy and criticism has dramatically shifted the rules of "doing good business," and global marketing organizations must evolve to address new challenges and opportunities. The assumption of responsibility and the adoption of greater transparency are now critical to how any brand or business plays its proper role in society. This new way of working represents a global revolution in marketing objectives and possibilities.

Morten Albæk characterizes this new way of thinking by describing it as "the intersection of capitalism and humanism." He adds, "These projects go beyond CSR; they represent new business models. The role of marketing is still to create future demand for products and services. Today, marketing also drives new programs for new generations. Marketers must be at the forefront of the business--thinking 5, 10 or even 15 years ahead of the sales cycle."

At the core of Morten Albæk's corporate philosophy is a belief in the necessity of creating an "enlightenment economy" as the antithesis to the "experience economy" and in merging capitalism and humanism (the two "isms" that have dominated Western culture for more than 500 years) into what he describes as a new "capitalistic humanistic innovation platform" to serve as an ideological frame for creating sustainable change.

He explains: "This means that innovation needs to do two things at the same time: generate the highest possible revenue and the highest possible EBIT, and, concurrently, have a positive societal impact. This is fully doable. This new platform is not 'humanistic capitalism,' because that would start with a utopia like creating world peace. Instead, by putting 'capitalism' before 'humanism', you add realism to ideals. And it is a fundamentally realistic ideal to change the energy mix by 2050."

This new 'capitalistic humanistic innovative platform' creates solutions that were indefinable in the old world. WindMade™ is one such example. Designed to unlock the potential for wind energy among global consumer brands, WindMade™ was created by Albæk with a coalition of global partners as the world's first global consumer label for a single energy source and the first ever label to be endorsed by the United Nations. In November 2011, he received an award from the American Wind Energy Association for the initiative, calling WindMade™ "probably the most unique communication initiative for wind in 30 years". Albæk's vision is to help consumers make an emotional connection with wind and equate the products they purchase with the type of renewable energy used to produce it.

"No corporation has ever jumped to the very beginning of the innovation chain and said, 'Why wait for consumers to demand a global consumer label for renewable energy?' He adds, "Why can't a corporation drive that innovation? Why can't a corporation create an NGO and hand it back to civil society? Doesn't social responsibility now mean stepping in and truly acting like a citizen? That gives me hope that if my 8-year old son is invited to a panel in 2050, when he's 44, he won't sit there and feel like his dad wasted his time."

According to Albæk, "We are in desperate need of a new social vision– one that insists that freedom and prosperity are contingent on the transparent use of reason." He believes corporations– no matter the industry– can build their business through doing greater good, and is a strong global voice on marketing transparency as an influential driver to achieving this goal.

He acknowledges that Vestas and the wind industry will never have the financial resources of their oil, coal and gas siblings, so he works to be innovative and aggressive in his positioning of the company and industry. He also encourages his marketing peers to increasingly think like "business developers," not "promoters."

Morten Albæk would counsel his fellow marketers that taking risks on big ideas pays huge dividends.

Without question, he is a CMO who advocates pushing boundaries as he strives to re-define notions of traditional marketing. Additional examples of marketing innovation at Vestas include the *Corporate Renewable Energy Index* (CREX) — the world's first renewable energy index and the largest mapping to date of global corporations' renewable energy procurement in collaboration with Bloomberg and the *Global Consumer Wind Study* — the most extensive global survey of consumers' preference for use of wind energy. Both are innovative concepts created to break down barriers for wind energy investments and demonstrate how Vestas, as the industry leader, takes responsibility for building the core market.

Vestas' *Energy Transparency* campaign has also broken new ground as a one-of-a-kind marketing effort, targeting Carbon Conscious Corporations by encouraging 622 top executives at global brands to invest directly in wind. Many were exposed to print ads or outdoor billboards close to their offices with custom-tailored messages that raised a few smiles and also some eyebrows. LinkedIn also played an integral part of the campaign, marking the first time a company used a social media platform to engage in one-to-one dialogue.

"My approach to marketing," he says, "is rooted in transparency, the power of facts, inclusiveness and dialog, along with unique and customized communication." He adds, "Mankind is born sensible and will act, react, and prioritize sensibly if only presented with insight and facts. Citizens and consumers have long been perceived apart. In today's interconnected society, the roles have merged. Citizens are slowly becoming aware of the impact that corporations have on the development of a prosperous society; consumers are aware that, via their purchasing decisions, they can influence how corporations act. That is why, instead of talking about citizens and consumers, I just talk about Citizumer's. It is just a matter of time before this new "figure" starts to move and a paradigm shift will emerge. CMOs not looking ahead will leave their brands behind."

When asked about the challenges of marketing multi-nationally today, he admits, "There are both internal and external challenges to overcome when creating a message that captures your audience across the globe. Internal alignment is paramount for consistent messaging, but yet, the message has to be localized to make a true impact. These are the reasons why I am a strong believer in one-to-one marketing using alternative channels, in building global collaborations and partnerships, and in integrating marketing with CSR, PR, sustainability and even philanthropy as a catalyst for effective business development."

He adds, "I know that it sounds banal but I want to use my life to change the world and marketing enables me to create something that has never been created before, something unique enough to inspire people to think, innovate, act, and react differently.

What wind companies have that other business-to-business organizations' don't, is they're selling a piece of technology that's going to save the world. Wind companies — including Vestas, until recently — are introverted, technology-driven beasts with little interest in or understanding of how they are perceived beyond their core customer base. (Considering how many smart and skillful people actually work in the wind business, I think the conservatism in the way we promote wind is mind-blowing!)

Of course, it would be nice if millions and millions of citizens were attached to the Vestas brand, and really thought it was something unique and inspiring. But, at the end of the day, what is truly important is that consumers are emotionally attached to wind.

My vision is to make Vestas one of the most customer-centric business-to-business-to-consumers organizations in the world. It is to help consumers make an emotional connection with wind and equate the products they purchase with the type of renewable energy used to produce it.

No doubt, he will achieve it.

Morten Albæk does not have a typical marketing background. He began his career as an academic with a focus History and Philosophy—both disciplines have served him well in creating a modern marketing organization based on a unique combination of responsibilities and a somewhat non-Scandinavian management philosophy.

He started his career in Danske Bank, Denmark's largest financial corporation, heading the department for Idea Generation and Innovation. There he pioneered the Financial Literacy Program. Lending itself to the same transparency and power of facts as Vestas initiatives, Albæk received the honor of having the case published in the UN Global Compact's yearbook, making him the first person ever to have two cases published in the same yearbook for two different companies.

Today he is CMO and Group Senior Vice President for Global Marketing, Communication & Corporate Relations of global wind turbine manufacturer Vestas Wind Systems, and part of Executive Management with direct CEO report.

Albæk has, as the only Scandinavian ever, been selected 4 times for The Internationalist's list of the "100 Most Influential CMOs in the World", one of "18 Global Champions" (in 2011), one of "50 Global Marketing Leaders" (in 2012), "Global Thought Leader" by the renewable industry's global magazine Recharge (in 2013), and part of Fast Company's list of the "1,000 most creative people in business" (in 2014). He was also named an **Internationalist of the Year** *in 2011.*

Albæk's marketing responsibilities extend to include green field development of a strategy for selling to emerging corporate customers such as IKEA, Google, Microsoft, etc. resulting in +250 million EUR revenue to date.

In addition to his professional merits, Albæk is an Honoree Professor in Philosophy at Aalborg University and a prominent character in the public debate about society related subjects. He is the author of three bestseller books "Generation Fucked Up?", "Encounters Between What You Say and What You Do" and "The Average Human Being" published in June 2013.

LEADERSHIP:
New Views of
Marketing Leadership

Nadine Karp McHugh

Talks about Creative Problem-Solving and Change Leadership to Navigate a New Marketing World

Nadine Karp McHugh
*Vice President of Global Integrated
Media Communications*
Colgate Palmolive
New York, New York USA

FAST FACTS
Where were you born?
Queens NY

What is the best advice you were ever given?
The best advice I was ever given was from my dad. At a young age he used to always ask me what I wanted to be when I grew up—it didn't matter what I answered (and the answer changed all the time). His answer, on the other hand, was always the same: "You can be anything you want to be as long as you work hard for it, just make sure you are happy." I grew up believing that I could be anything I wanted to be, and now realize that I checked my professional decisions on whether or not I would be happy. It has been my internal barometer and has guided me through many decisions. I have learned that being happy in most of the positions I have taken over the years has made all the difference in the world in how you approach your job every day. This way of thinking has also nurtured my passion and skills in creative thinking and my belief that anything is possible—as long as you are willing to work hard to create it.

What was your big career break?
I worked at WPP for 20 plus years....The first break was getting my first job there at Ogilvy & Mather as a Media Planner. I also ran the Unilever US business when the function of Communications Planning was being developed in the US. I was able to help shape what that looked like for their 30+ brands at the time. Running the NY office of Mindshare was my last position at WPP in the middle of the last recession. All of these positions were great learning experiences at different levels and for many reasons

What's your favorite city for business travel?
There are so many!!! Bangkok, London, Paris, Mumbai…

What's your favorite place in the world?
Italy—hands down, but lots of close seconds--Switzerland, France, Turks and Caicos.

NADINE KARP MCHUGH IS COMMITTED TO THE DEMOCRATIZATION OF MARKETING. With more than two decades of devotion to media, communications planning, strategy, solutions, management and training, she believes that marketing will only continue to become more complex as technology changes the way we approach consumers, and more importantly, changes the way consumers engage with content and brands.

Not only does this increased complexity excite her, it has inspired her to take action to help lead the change.

As Vice President of Global Integrated Media Communications at Colgate Palmolive®, a global company serving more than 200 countries and territories with consumer products that make lives healthier and more enjoyable—McHugh is responsible for driving best-in-class digitized media and integrated marketing ideas and best practices. She encourages excellence in a wide diversity of brands-- including Colgate® toothpastes, Speed Stick®, Irish Spring® , Palmolive® and Hill's Pet Nutrition's line of pet foods.

Without question, Nadine has a passion for high caliber creative problem-solving that drives brands to find distinctive "own-able" solutions, particularly ones that ultimately result in competitive advantage. She firmly believes that the future of marketing will depend on everyone's ability to harness their creative potential to drive and build "the possible." For her, this is the democratization of marketing to which she is so unwaveringly committed.

She adds, "Technology has changed our world and will continue to do so in ways we have not yet dreamed of. By thinking differently and being able to reframe problems, the future we create is only as limited as we allow it to be."

Nadine's own history in the industry has shaped her belief in the critical importance of navigating in a new marketing world. Not only has she been a pioneer in many emerging sectors of marketer and agency solutions, but she decided to devote her late nights and weekends to completing a Master's degree, remotely and through annual on-site work (aka Grad School Boot Camp), in an entirely new field. In fact, just this spring she was the world's 500th graduate with a Master's of Science in Creativity and Change Leadership.

She says, "I felt that getting this additional degree was a great way to arm myself, and the businesses I support, with the confidence and expertise needed to move forward in our ever-changing world. Creative problem-solving and change-management leadership are among the credentials now necessary to transform businesses so they can better steer toward the future, and the global world of marketing and communications must be at the forefront."

Her Master's degree comes from the International Center for Studies in Creativity (ICSC), part of the State University of New York in Buffalo, which boasts the oldest creative studies program in the world, with course offerings on creativity since 1967. In addition to graduate programs and an undergraduate minor in the discipline, ICSC is currently planning for a Ph.D. program. No word yet if Nadine is tempted to go further in her studies.

She explains, "It all began with Alex Osborn, one of the founders of BBDO, who was also the father of brainstorming." As one would suspect, the program focuses on using innate creativity to find new solutions, yet in doing so, it sets up a framework for empowering others within an organization to have the confidence to use new tools. According to Nadine, "the future of business is increasingly about the balance of analytics and creativity. I want to be sure that I am thinking in such a way that I can harness what is available to construct relevant solutions and productive change."

She admits, "A large part of the course work is studying and practicing models and frameworks that provide opportunities for people to 'own' their own creativity. What organization wouldn't want to infuse this kind of thinking into its processes? This is becoming a movement around the world. We often talk about right brain and left brain, and the potential of big data infused with creativity. Where they meet, will be where the magic happens."

In February, The New York Times' Education Life section featured an article on Nadine's Master's Program, aptly titled: "Learning to Think Outside the Box. Creativity Becomes an Academic Discipline."

The story cites Dr. Gerard Puccio, Chairman of the International Center for Studies in Creativity in Buffalo as saying, "The reality is that to survive in a fast-changing world you need to be creative. That is why you are seeing more attention to creativity at universities. The marketplace is demanding it."

He continues, "Critical thinking has long been regarded as the essential skill for success, but it's not enough. Creativity moves beyond mere synthesis and evaluation, and is 'the higher order skill.'"

According to *The New York Times*, this has not been a sudden development. Apparently, two decades ago, "creating" replaced "evaluation" at the top of Bloom's Taxonomy, the educational system that classifies learning objectives for students. More recently, in 2010, an IBM survey of 1,500 chief executives in 33 industries determined that "creativity" was considered the most essential factor to success. And in our contemporary world, LinkedIn found that "creative" has been the most-used buzzword in their members' profiles for the past two years.

As a result, "creativity" is becoming a work credential, and Creative Studies is increasingly appearing on academic course lists. These programs, sometimes considered "transdisciplinary," are found as new options in business, education, digital media, humanities, arts, science and engineering programs.

Interestingly, creativity was once assumed to be the mark of divine inspiration, the call of a muse, or the amazing flash of genius. From an academic standpoint, it is increasingly being seen in a more egalitarian light, and as a discipline that takes skill, not magic. This is a huge change. Creativity is now viewed as the ability to recognize problems or reframe challenges, and then develop intelligent or transformative solutions. As a result, creativity, at least in this definition, is considered a greatly valued, yet teachable and practical "process skill," crucial to mastering fast-change, overwhelming choice, and often great ambiguity.

Nadine notes that a requirement of the Master's project was to create something that would drive productive change. She chose to develop a Creative DNA Guide for Business. "This guide," she says, "supports the idea that everyone has the potential and the right to think creatively. In today's world, being able to embrace one's creative potential and leverage it is required if we are to succeed."

She adds, "Even in our new era of real-time big data, smart marketers need to be able to capture the insights that result from this data to find "own-able" and unique solutions that will make a difference. Everyone is talking about big data driving everything— and it will—but without insights and creative problem-solving, it cannot be effective. Data is just a blunt tool waiting to be sharpened."

When considering today's challenges to progress in our industry, Nadine says, "Much could be accomplished through greater collaboration, so that we can all move forward faster. Silos help no one. Those who can move dynamically through the future will win."

Her Master's project, combined with her current role at Colgate-Palmolive and her past work with agencies, media, and brands, has caused her to think deeply about the possibilities that stem from dramatic change. Nadine often talks about one of the biggest shifts in her marketing experience: "There is an ongoing sense that nothing will ever be the same. I think it is wonderful, because it opens up so many possibilities. Essentially, if you can imagine something, you can find a way to create it-- technology has made this so. This DEMOCRATIZES marketing! You no longer need to be the brand with the biggest budget. Instead, the most compelling, engaging and relevant story can win."

She often speaks of 2013 Cannes winner, Holland's Dela Funeral Insurance. The company's "Why Wait Till It's Too Late" campaign, created by Ogilvy & Mather Amsterdam, is an example of this democratization. Nadine believes that the campaign literally made the impossible happen. She says, "Through a terrific, integrated marketing campaign, the brand, a Funeral Insurance Company becomes life hero by reminding people to celebrate their loved ones while they're still here—a departure from the usual business of Funeral Insurance."

The campaign encouraged people to express their thanks to living family members and friends. The messages were shared across a span of media—ranging from online messages to outdoor ads placed where the loved ones would see them. Dela even took over a news broadcast and invited people to say thank you to those they loved on live television. Of course, the campaign's goal was to inspire the people of Holland to buy more funeral insurance from Dela, while also increasing brand recognition. The campaign was a business success; Dela reported that its amount of insured capital grew by 50%.

Nadine emphasizes, "If funeral insurance can accomplish the extraordinary via media communications, the rest of us should be encouraged to do great things that are truly inspirational."

So how is Nadine Karp McHugh helping to reshape marketing? "In our current state of constant transition, my goal is to drive productive change-- not change simply for the sake of change. I find it satisfying to identify the game changers and then share those insights throughout the company to make a difference. This was my sweet spot on the agency side, and is something I am enjoying in my current position.

I tend to go towards the fire, when many are not as lured by the flame. My hope is that through my new Master's experience I can effectively encourage the type of on-going productive change needed in media communications to establish competitive advantage today and into the future."

Prior to joining Colgate-Palmolive in 2011, McHugh was a Senior Marketing Executive at WPP/GroupM's Mindshare and Managing Director of the New York office with responsibility for all clients—both local and global. Her deep experience in building successful consumer-based integrated marketing and media programs and communications frameworks have enabled her to work across an amazing variety of categories, including Consumer Packaged Goods, Beauty, Fashion, Food, Skin Care, Fragrances, Telecommunications, QSR, Home Electronics, Financial, Entertainment and Travel.

Before assuming the Mindshare New York M/D role, Nadine also managed the Unilever US business. As part of the Mindshare Global Unilever Executive Committee, she oversaw how best practices and key initiatives were developed globally. As a key member of the core integrated marketing team that helped elevate Unilever's game, she served as the Communications Planner and Client Lead on the award winning "In The Motherhood" webisode series and integrated marketing program—a first of its kind and a Cannes Media Lions Winner. Nadine also played a key role on the global Dove Masterbrand integrated team, and helped create never-been-done-before programs and consumer experiences that grew Dove from a beauty bar into the extraordinary success it is today.

She is also personally committed to training and raising the bar on Communications Planning. Her 15+ years of training experience, which include develop-

ing training programs and an entire curriculum, embraced a reverse-mentoring program to help educate, empower, and "digitize" senior staff.

In 2014, The Internationalist named Nadine one of its Top 100 Marketing Leaders. This list recognizes accomplished executives who are using their experience, insights and expanded responsibilities to develop new marketing solutions amid today's global complexity and redefined business objectives. In 2012, Nadine was named as a Top Innovator by Brand Innovators for her contributions in driving creative innovative media solutions. In 2009, Advertising Age named Nadine a "Media Maven" for her breakthrough thinking and creative approach as well as her success in driving effective storytelling initiatives across the Mindshare culture and businesses. Also in 2009, Nadine received an "Impact" award from Advertising Women of New York for her mentoring efforts. In 2008, Nadine was named an "Advertising Working Mother of the Year" by the Advertising Women of New York, a recognition that honors the most successful working mothers in advertising and media, while in 2006, she was named one of Advertising Age's "Women to Watch," a distinction that illustrated her growing reputation and stature in national marketing and media.

At the time of printing, Nadine Karp McHugh announced that she will take on a new role this autumn as Senior Vice President Omnimedia, Strategic Investments and Creative Solutions for L'Oreal USA. Without doubt that her new creativity and change leadership beliefs will benefit this multinational marketer, too.

Jesper Colding

Originally from Denmark, Leads One of China's Key Companies to Become a Brand Building Organization

Jesper Colding
Vice President
Mengniu Dairy Company China
Hohhot, Inner Mongolia &
Beijing, China

FAST FACTS
Where were you born?
Copenhagen, Denmark

Was there a lesson you learned in an early first job that still applies now?
I started as a sales trainee at P&G. Monday mornings, I'd get up very and early and merchandise Pampers in a hyper-market chain. It was humbling, yet satisfying to go right from business school onto the shop floor. It was very real, hands-on, and the importance of the store and the shopper fundamentals has never left me.

What is the best advice you were ever given?
Get and stay uncomfortable.

What was your big career break?
Joining P&G as an intern in 1994.

What's your favorite city for business travel?
Hong Kong or Paris for the food.

What's your favorite place in the world?
Remote places with my family. If I should one, then the small island of Sangalaki in Indonesia on the east coast of Borneo. A diving place almost out of operation. A bumpy ride to get there. We were the only guests on the small island. Every night, turtles would dig nest in the sand, and every morning turtles would hatch. Diving was beautiful.

INNER MONGOLIA IS A VERY LONG WAY FROM DENMARK, but Jesper Fournaise Colding doesn't mind. True to his Viking roots, he's an adventurer and an internationalist who has lived and worked in eight countries over the past two decades, including a 13-year career with Procter & Gamble in the Nordic region, as well as in Southeast Asia. Even his education was multinational with an undergraduate degree in Macro Economics from Southern Denmark University and a Masters in International Marketing from both Southern Denmark University and the University of Denver in the United States.

Other stops along the way have included a role as General Manager of Danish Brewery Royal Unibrew in the Baltics—a region where the company has a strong presence, and Senior Vice President of Global Categories and Operations at Arla Foods, the Swedish-Danish cooperative that is not only Scandinavia's largest producer of dairy products, but also the 7th largest diary company in the world as measured by turnover.

His role at Arla paved the way to join Inner Mongolia Mengniu, a subsidiary of China Mengniu Dairy Company Limited established in 1999 and headquartered in the provincial capital of Hohhot, where he is responsible for managing the marketing division. His arrival coincides with Mengniu's desire to both improve product safety and rebuild consumer trust in the aftermath of well-known tainted food scares in China.

Several acquisitions and partnerships are working to insure that the company has greater control over the source of its milk supply, as well as access to better food safety technology. It acquired Yashili, a Chinese infant formula maker that sources largely from New Zealand. Mengniu, as China's largest dairy producer, now also enjoys joint ventures with-

France's Danone, as well as with Arla Foods. These partnerships provide the Chinese company with technology in exchange for distribution for the Europeans.

Yet, Mengniu 's new Executive Director & CEO Ms. Sun Yiping also understood that it needed a new CMO to lead a separate sales and marketing operation to transform the company into an effective brand-building organization—without losing its entrepreneurial culture. (Mengniu was started 15 years earlier by several individuals inspired by the potential for China's new future. Marketing had previously aligned under sales in three separate divisions—i) chilled products ii) UHT products and iii) ice cream. Ms. Sun merged the business into one entity and then separated sales and marketing. There was no CMO role prior to this change.)

Jesper Colding was a perfect fit given his P&G training, his understanding of dairy through Arla, and his experience in the region. Plus, his wife is Malaysian-Chinese, which provided him with additional cultural familiarity. He adds that he was "truly honored that such a passionate Chinese company would accept a foreigner in so essential a role." He says that his only regret is that he not yet adopted the language sufficiently. "It allows for depth and understanding when you're that close to the culture." (Whereas his six-year-old is fluent in English and Danish, and making strong progress in Chinese.) He finds China fascinating, and appreciates the intense working environment. He says, "It is a different work-life balance than I have experienced before. There is family and work-family; it really blends together. The work ethic is amazing."

Jesper's appointment followed the arrival of a new Executive Director & CEO for Mengniu—a woman—Ms. Sun Yiping, to whom he reports, who was educated in both China and the US. Ms. Sun has extensive management experience in real estate, as well as fast-moving consumer goods. Her career started at COFCO, the largest supplier in China's agricultural products and food industry, where she was involved in the management of COFCO's investment in the Coca-Cola bottling business. Other roles included deputy general manager of Swire Guangdong Coca-Cola Limited, general manager of Hainan Coca-Cola Beverages Co., and general manager of Zhanjiang COFCO Coca-Cola Beverages Ltd. COFCO plays a pivotal role in the markets of edible oils and foodstuff between China and the world, and serves as the main importing and exporting channel for bulk agricultural products. Mengniu is one of the companies in the COFCO portfolio.

Interestingly, in an address to shareholders by Ms. Sun Yiping, Jesper Colding was discussed. After explaining why his experience was of great value to Mengniu, she also made reference to his height in comparison to his Chinese colleagues. Ms. Sun added, "He shows us that drinking milk since a young age can help you grow tall." The comment strengthened Jesper's resolve to insure that the company would also grow.

Although he worked in Asia before, he notes the Mengniu was "a 100% Chinese environment with no English." He insists that one can only experience such a situation to fully understand the range of implications. However, he's found the process wonderfully positive. Jesper says he was "cloned with simultaneous translators from the beginning." He also explains that there is very little email in the company as most daily conversations are via WeChat. Given the short nature of WeChat, he can quickly and easily translate most messages. "It works surprisingly well. We have a Top 6 Group, a Top 50 Group, and everything is quick and efficient. It's a level of connectivity that I have not experienced before, and should extend beyond Chinese companies."

He admits that it was immediately clear to him what needed to be done. Mengniu was built on milk, processing, and a superior distribution network. It had begun to build brand strength through an increasing penetration of dairy sales. (Dairy was a new food group for China; the traditional Chinese diet didn't include much milk, cheese, yogurt or ice cream.) Although the category was growing through habit, usage, and frequency of purchase, Mengniu still needed to move from marketing a vast array of products to essential, yet tailored brand-building.

Plus, the company attracted some of the foremost talent in China with capabilities in agricultural products, food processing, equipment and engineering. Jesper needed strong marketing directors to provide Mengniu with the best of a new corporate architecture, while creating the necessary alignment for all possible stakeholders.

When Jesper joined the company, Mengniu had more than 50 brands and "a very long SKU trail." Now the dairy maker concentrates on 15 brands with a clearer focus and with an eye toward delivering for the future. The company is working to communicate more directly with customers with a tagline of "A little happiness matters," while also organizing its brands into clearly-defined sectors.

According to Jesper Colding, "Product development and branding in the past had been either category or product focused in groupings like milk ice cream, and yogurt. That has now shifted. Mengniu today thinks about issues like: 'What is motivating the consumption of dairy?' This is a tremendous change for someone who is an ice cream brand manager, for example. They will think about whether they are in the indulgence business or the nutrition business. Their new issues revolve around understanding volume and profit pools, so that they can be better targeted when considering new forms of innovation. This fundamental change allows us to think strategically against a platform instead of being in a vast product space."

He adds philosophically that "all brands consume resources." So focus and a concentration of resources do matter.

Even while based in China, Jesper observes that marketing throughout the world is moving from striving for mass influence to advocacy. Yet he comments that many companies still have a tendency to think mass even with digital advertising and online TV. "Few have cracked the code on how to really engage in ways that really matter to consumers—from content for the day to longer-term relationships. It's so easy for consumers to shut you out. Everyone is scratching at the surface of meaningful engagement."

He admits that if you're a senior marketing today, you still have DNA that's most comfortable with traditional media. "And most of marketing is still traditional. Digital is largely about two things. The first is screens, and an iPad or tablet still can provide the same 15: spot on a smaller-sized screen, so it's not so different from the past. The second is real-time, social engagement. This is still largely new territory with few successful models or best practices on how to make an impact."

He also talks about how he is working to market effectively in a country that is largely digital. He calls his efforts "early in the learning curve." Yet, he has enormous respect for media companies like Tencent and Baidu. "If you want to engage with them, they are unquestionably providing a new type of model-- never seen before. I'd call it 'a mega media outline' in that they provide platforms with consumers, data and all forms of research available to a partner, as well as production capability. Essentially, they have everything under the same hood, which certainly challenges the old agency-client-media relationships. This new model is emerging fast, and, frankly, I'm impressed by their overall engagement with consumers."

"Every marketer," he says, "wants a *relationship* with the consumer— from makers of toilet paper to fashion companies to the car business. Yet, the consumer doesn't really want a relationship with everyone. It's actually okay not to engage everywhere with everybody. Instead, we, as marketers, should focus on who at what level, and how they care. Perhaps these are the basics of good corporate citizenship; however, to show you are a caring company today is essential, and this must continue."

Jesper believes that "brands enable consumers to experience a huge spectrum of just what they care about. In the past, we had communications messages. Now we must create inspirational brands. Consumers no longer 'consume' a brand; they instead connect to what they care about through the brand. This is the new matrix for the future."

Speaking of the future, Jesper Colding is also certain that many Chinese companies will soon start moving outside of China. "Innovation here is truly mind blowing, and it now goes beyond manufacturing. My small contribution here, today, is that I grew up in the developed world with mature marketing tools, so I can help bring that context to China.However, what China is teaching me in terms of appetite, speed and innovation makes it clear that I am getting impacted more than I am impacting. It is very humbling and unsettling, but it also provides extraordinary inspiration."

Jesper Colding is now transitioning to a new role in Mengniu, where he will head Strategy and M&A, while continuing to report to the CEO in a Vice President capacity. The move is a natural evolution of his work in the past two years to help Mengniu establish a marketing foundation and direction. He will hand over those responsibilities—at the right moment—to enable further acceleration of marketing's effects for Mengniu.

Before joining Inner Mongolia Mengniu he was the Senior Vice President of Arla Foods in Global Categories and Operations from September 2009.

From January 2007 he worked as the General Manager of Royal Unibrew Baltic countries, a leading beer and beverage company in the region.

From 1994 to 2007, Mr. Colding had taken various roles within sales/marketing in P&G and worked in leading roles in Denmark, Sweden, and Norway before he worked as an Associate Director in P&G Malaysia/Singapore.

He has extensive experience in sales/marketing and general management and a record of building strong organizations and results. Mr. Colding obtained a Bachelor's degree in Macro Economics and a Master of International Marketing from Southern Denmark University and Denver University in USA.

*Jesper Colding was named an **Internationalist of the Year** in 2013.*

Joe Tripodi

of Coca-Cola
Discusses the New
Ideals of
Marketing Leadership

Joseph V. Tripodi
Chief Marketing & Commercial Officer
The Coca-Cola Company
Atlanta, Georgia USA

FAST FACTS
Where were you born?
Miami Beach, Florida.

Was there a lesson you learned in an early first job that still applies now?
Challenge convention and don't believe your own BS.

What is the best advice you were ever given?
My parents told me never to judge people by the color of their skin, their religion, their appearance or the size of their wallet.

What was your big career break?
Being hired by Pete Hart at MasterCard to lead international marketing.

Are you willing to admit your biggest career mistake? (Or at least the one you learned the most from!)
Absolutely. Many mistakes. Biggest learning is that speed always trumps perfection.

Where do you turn for inspiration?
My three teenagers. They keep me humble and remind me how little I know.

What's your favorite city for business travel?
Hong Kong

What's your favorite place in the world?
South of France.

WITHOUT QUESTION, JOE TRIPODI UNDER-
STANDS THE INTEGRAL ROLE that brands play within
the overall cultural landscape. Whether Coca-Cola's
first advertising campaign, *The Pause that Refreshes*
in the 1920s ... or *Things Go Better with Coke* in the
'60s ... or today's *Open Happiness* — these brand sen-
timents touch people, spark emotions and memories,
and can even impart a very specific sense of time, place
and social relevance. He also knows that as the world's
most-recognized and most-valuable brand, Coca-Cola
has a position in the global cultural consciousness.

As the Marketing and Commercial leader for the world's largest
beverage company, Joe also recognizes the need to adapt to the ideals
of new audiences, while creating internal and external structures that
reflect a changing world. In the process, he has not only played a pivotal role in the reinvention of marketing, but has actually changed the
definition and requirements of contemporary marketing leadership par
excellence.

Few individuals have been able to embrace so many elements
of today's marketing complexity, while also reevaluating an effective
global structure, and inspiring idealism within a company and a worldwide community of customers.   Joe has not only managed to keep a
128-year-old flagship brand at the top of its game, but is committed to
driving an aggressive growth mission. Coca-Cola's 2020 Vision, announced by CEO Muhtar Kent in 2009, sets the bar for the company and
its bottling partners to double their collective revenues to $200 billion
by the end of the decade. (Yes, this means generating the same amount
of sales in this decade as Coca-Cola had built in its first 125 years.)

Not only does Joe Tripodi believe that this immense goal is do-able, he's clear about the process: "The only way we're going to achieve this is through innovations across our system." This means broadly engaging the entire Coke ecosystem of people and organizations by staying relevant, by keeping the brand familiar, and by evoking true cultural leadership. He adds, "New rules and opportunities require courage, risk, and reinvention on all of our parts. This is not limited to how we go to market. We have to reinvent our company and the way we are structured and networked."

As a result, he has focused his energies on two critical areas that, together, have now proven to drive excellence. One is mastering the new mechanics of marketing—achieved through understanding Millennial values and engagement, a "liquid and linked" content strategy, grooming a new generation of creative talent, and recognizing the role of creativity in an era of Big Data. The other is encouraging effective, world class leadership by building a networked marketing organization, using the role of CMO and Commercial Leader as the catalyst for new strategic direction and enterprise change, and championing the higher purpose of brands and marketing through thought leadership, as well as cultural leadership.

For most, this would be an exceptionally tall order, and Joe admits it is not easy—even for the world's most-recognized brand and a huge multinational corporation with over 700,000 system associates world-wide and a market cap of $180+ billion. But Joe Tripodi and Coca-Cola take the responsibilities of leadership seriously. He says, "It is our ability to adapt, to participate in, and even lead in culture that will allow us to achieve our business goals."

By the numbers, the Coca-Cola Corporation is staggering—distribution in 200+ countries, relationships with over 24 million retail outlets, and 3500+ products, including such well-known brands as Minute Maid,

Fanta, Sprite, Fresca, Dr. Pepper, Schweppes, FUZE, Odwalla, DASANI, glacéau smartwater, and new players like Honest Tea and Monster, as well as local favorites like Inca Kola in Peru, Minute Maid Pulpy in China, Apollinaris in Germany, Rani in the Middle East, I Lohas and Georgia Coffee in Japan, and Stoney Ginger Beer in South Africa. The company is a global trailblazer in sodas, juice, waters, enhanced waters, sports drinks, as well as ready-to-drink coffee and tea.

The Coca-Cola Company's mission may be to refresh the world, inspire moments of happiness, and make a difference, yet Joe asserts that the brand must "evoke happiness, not plant a flag and expect people to rally around it."

Although very much aware of the world's galloping demographics of greater urbanization, growing middle classes and an accelerated pace of change, he asserts that "demographics are not destiny" for any mass brand today. He says, "Every 30 days, a new Atlanta is added to the world, but a brand still has to capture new consumers. We have to engage our market, and understand that our culture is participatory."

Interestingly, for a brand as globally ubiquitous as Coca-Cola, Joe Tripodi admits that there is a powerful level beyond "global" today that must be embraced. "Business has evolved. It's not enough to go from local to multi-country to global anymore. The next step is the 'networked organization.' Today you have to be networked through 'nodes' or localized sensors and 'hubs' or centers of excellence, so you put brands at the center of the conversation." He adds, "It's no longer about the size of your budget, but the size of your idea."

So what is a Networked Organization? Joe often begins by explaining what it is not. "A networked organization is not a siloed corporation executing against a long-term strategy that assumes certainties and variables in the marketplace." He believes that today's world teaches us that there are few certainties and we can no longer assume all the variables. In fact, flexibility is the only way to keep up with the pace of change.

Joe characterizes the Networked Organization as breaking with a traditional corporate structure to create more flexibility for individuals to adapt to change and opportunity. "It is a learning organization, and a willingness to take risks on a daily basis is part of the culture. Success and failure are shared throughout the organization. Centers of excellence scale better work around the world, with less redundancy." At its heart are three principles:

1. To be nimble in a dynamic marketplace.

2 To manage the evolution of the organization with the evolution of the marketplace.

3. To be an adaptive culture, not a stagnant one.

There are two elements to a Networked Organization-- the internal network of Coca-Cola employees and bottlers through the world and the external network of customers, governments, influencers, opinion leaders, investors, rights holders, academia, NGOs and the media.

Together, internal and external networks represent shared value for the brand; both are critical to overall growth and success. According to Joe, "Coca-Cola has found that when it uses our Networked Organization to support our global marketplace, our value chain partners and our world, we see exponential return."

"Ultimately," he says, "our goal is to deliver to people on their terms, not ours. This is a complete paradigm shift. We ask ourselves-- How can we reimagine all of our assets… coolers, trucks, kiosks, to be digitally networked to facilitate a two-way conversation between our brands and the people buying them? This is now a question for every industry."

He adds, "By creating a shared value platform, everyone can become an agent for positive change in the world." Joe Tripodi also clearly understands that Coca-Cola's future is tied to growing sustainably, and considers it a core part of the company's shared values with its broad ecosystem. For example, issues relating to clean water are essential to a beverage company, and they also contribute to the shared values of NGOs and community leaders in places as diverse as India and Kenya.

One of new Coca-Cola ideas for global responsibility is the EKO-CENTER™, announced at The Clinton Global Initiative in 2012. (The name incorporates both ecology and the spelling of "Coke" backwards.) At the heart of the EKOCENTER™ is the Slingshot™ water purification system that can support 300 people per day. Nearly 60% of all diseases in the poorest socio-economic communities originate from impure water.

To help provide communities in need with access to safe drinking water and other basic necessities, The Coca-Cola Company and other partners, including development banks and NGOs, launched EKOCEN-TER™—a community center in a box, complete with a water purification system. The EKOCENTER project aims to improve the holistic well-being of developing communities around the world, focusing on those within the Bottom of the Pyramid (BoP), or nearly 4 billion people around the globe who live on less than US$2 per day.

The Slingshot water purification system uses vapor compression distillation (VCD) technology to turn any source of dirty water—river water, ocean water and even raw sewage—into safe, clean drinking water. The technology, developed by inventor and DEKA R&D President Dean Kamen, delivers approximately 800 liters of clean water daily at the hourly electricity cost of less than a standard handheld hair dryer (1kWh).

Another well-known example of how cultural leadership plays a role in creating a network advantage is the polar bear. Given how the bear is intrinsically tied to Coca-Cola's image, the company worked with the World Wildlife Fund to raise millions of dollars and significantly increase awareness of the animal's plight through a wonderfully innovative idea.

Coke turned over a billion cans from classic red to polar white for a 6-week period to draw attention to the great bear and its habitat. The striking white cans stood out in a sea of iconic Coca-Cola red. According to Joe, "We could have written a check as a contribution, but we wanted to challenge ourselves in a different way to greater results and greater good."

Joe Tripodi constantly reinforces that marketers can lead a cultural dialogue for their brands. "Don't forget the power of advertising and communications. By insuring a brand is a force for good, it brings benefits to consumers, delivers shared value, and creates a network of advocates. If we don't evolve and change, we won't be successful. You don't have a choice. The people are taking you there."

He states, "Just a few years ago, we wanted to be the best in the world. We have now evolved our thinking to wanting to be the best FOR the world in ALL that we do across the Coca-Cola system. This is our new guiding principle."

Interestingly, this guiding principle also speaks to a global Millennial Generation. And this principle evolved, in large part, from Coca-Cola's strong commitment to understanding Millennial values and expectations. In fact, Joe is looking to the future through the eyes of Millennials throughout the world. He describes today's 18 to 30 year olds as the "we" generation, rather than past "me" generations. He says, "Disenchanted with the status quo, they are indeed changing the world."

To captivate dynamic Millennials throughout the globe, he describes a new framework of values with the acronym "TAOS" to represent Transparent, Authentic, Organic, and Sustainable. Coca-Cola is adopting these engagement strategies to innovate and evolve their marketing thinking, but the ideals has already proven to have significant implications for the company and even the globe.

Yes, Millennials may be digital natives, but Joe Tripodi also recognizes, "They expect unlimited choice-- personalized and delivered through multiple channels at maximum speed." Most importantly, he cites how Millennials are striving to change their world to align with a new set of values; increasingly the key to contemporary brand relevance is reflecting those values that Millennials cherish and respect. Thanks to modern technology, an individual now has the ability to influence opinion, start a movement, and affect change. To keep such dynamic consumers engaged, a brand must innovate, and Coca-Cola is focusing its power of innovation on packaging, partnerships, products & equipment, consumer provocations, and, of course, cultural leadership.

"Creativity," says Tripodi, "is essential to driving innovation and it's not limited to how Coke goes to market."

Increasingly in an age of design, more people are recognizing the value and effects of packaging. Coca-Cola's contour-shaped bottle will be 100 years old in 2015. With such an iconic shape so strong identified with the brand, experiments in packaging can be risky. Nonetheless, Coke experimented. In Australia, Coca-Cola created customized packaging by boldly replacing the brand name with popular Teen first names. Not only did sales soar, but Millennials were delighted and shared their wonder on social media.

This Share-A-Coke program is now available in 50+ markets. Coke even found solutions in countries where customization by name was not possible—such as Japan. Instead, they personalized via a partnership with Sony, so that consumers could download free songs from their birth year.

A wonderful new packaging innovation was the shareable can—initially launched in Singapore, where smaller portions are looked upon favorably. With a quick twist, a standard becomes two individual half servings. What could be the better embodiment of sharing happiness?

Another extraordinary innovation through manufacturing and equipment is the FreeStyle machine-- literally a next-generation fountain dispenser. Offering over 100 products, FreeStyle creates a myriad of flavor mixes, offering new, personalized flavor combinations. Not only is this another level of customization, but it represents a huge shift toward customer co-creation—again in line with Millennial expectations.

A mobile app also allows consumers to save their blends, so any Freestyle machine can create a preferred flavor combo. This real-time consumer co-creation also provides Coke with insights on product preferences and consumer engagement that could result in completely new segments and insights for the company.

Coca-Cola is also migrating from being a brand that promotes happiness, to a brand that provokes happiness. Its strategy on social platforms is to provoke experiences through powerful stories that are "shareworthy" enough to encourage conversation. Coke recognizes that in a world now reordered by Millennials, it has to engage in active conversations. Sometimes those conversations can be awkward, such as the subject of obesity.

According to Tripodi, "Our position as a cultural leader on this issue is our commitment to be part of the solution. We have developed a full 360 degree Engagement Plan." This includes low and no calorie beverages, transparent nutrition information, inspiring well-being while encouraging movement through support of physical activity programs, and a responsible marketing policy that stipulates No Advertising to children under the age of 12.

While technology is more and more an enabler or enhancer of experiences, Joe Tripodi still believes that "good marketing is about the soul of your brand." It requires passion, intellectual curiosity, risk-taking and cultural leadership. He warns that marketers should not be seduced